TWELFTH EDITION

CLASSROOM READING INVENTORY

WARREN H. WHEELOCK

University of Missouri–Kansas City

CONNIE J. CAMPBELL

Campbell-Wheelock Interventions, Inc.

CLASSROOM READING INVENTORY, TWELFTH EDITION

Published by McGraw-Hill, a business unit of The McGraw-Hill Companies, Inc., 1221 Avenue of the Americas, New York, NY 10020. Copyright © 2012 by The McGraw-Hill Companies, Inc. All rights reserved. Previous edition © 2009, 2004, and 1997. No part of this publication may be reproduced or distributed in any form or by any means, or stored in a database or retrieval system, without the prior written consent of The McGraw-Hill Companies, Inc., including, but not limited to, in any network or other electronic storage or transmission, or broadcast for distance learning.

Some ancillaries, including electronic and print components, may not be available to customers outside the United States.

This book is printed on recycled, acid-free paper containing 10% postconsumer waste.

1 2 3 4 5 6 7 8 9 0 QDB/QDB 1 0 9 8 7 6 5 4 3 2 1

ISBN 978-0-07-811025-2
MHID 0-07-811025-4

Vice President & Editor-in-Chief: *Michael Ryan*
Vice President EDP/Central Publishing Services: *Kimberly Meriwether David*
Publisher: *Beth Mejia*
Sponsoring Editor: *Allison McNamara*
Managing Editor: *Marley Magaziner*
Executive Marketing Manager: *Pamela S. Cooper*
Senior Project Manager: *Lisa A. Bruflodt*
Design Coordinator: *Margarite Reynolds*
Cover Designer: *Jenny Lindeman, Studio Montage*
Cover Image: *Royalty-Free/CORBIS*
Buyer: *Susan K. Culbertson*
Media Project Manager: *Sridevi Palani*
Compositor: *Laserwords Private Limited*
Typeface: *11/13 Times Roman*
Printer: *Quad/Graphics*

All credits appearing on page or at the end of the book are considered to be an extension of the copyright page.

Library of Congress Cataloging-in-Publication Data

Wheelock, Warren.
  Classroom reading inventory/Warren Wheelock, Nicholas Silvaroli, Connie Campbell.—12th ed.
    p. cm.
  ISBN 978-0-07-811025-2 (alk. paper)
  1. Reading—Ability testing. 2. Reading (Elementary) I. Silvaroli, Nicholas. II. Campbell, Connie. III. Title.
LB1050.46.S53 2011
372.48—dc22

2010034734

DEDICATION

Nicholas J. Silvaroli
1930–1995

*I count myself in nothing else so happy as in a
soul remembering my good friend.*

Wm. Shakespeare—King Richard II

CONTENTS

PREFACE

The Classroom Reading Inventory (CRI) is specially prepared for inservice teachers and preservice teachers who have little or no experience with informal reading inventories.

The CRI is a leading reading diagnostic tool because of its ease of use and time-saving administration. If you read the entire manual carefully and study the specific procedures thoroughly, you will gain the information to begin mastery of the CRI.

Get started with the basics by administering the CRI to at least three students. Your skill and success with individual diagnostic reading techniques are developed gradually through experience. You will find that the techniques, procedures and ideas must be adapted to each student and testing situation, for no two are alike.

After you administer the CRI seven to ten times, you will find yourself more and more adept in understanding, documenting and interpreting the reader's responses. Most important, you will see your teaching improve because you will align your instruction more clearly and precisely with the reading needs, levels, skills, and comprehension priorities of your students.

As with previous editions of the CRI, you will see that Form A follows a subskills format, and Form B follows a reader response format. Both forms include pretests and posttests.

What's New in This Edition?

We have made the following changes, additions, and modifications to this edition based on feedback from CRI users:

- **Multicultural stories and themes:** More than 20 percent of the stories are new and updated, with expanded emphasis on multicultural characters, global themes and high interest topics.
- **Online high school and adult testing material:** The diagnostic and subskills material for high school and adult education students continue to be available online at *www.classroomreadinginventory.com* in improved access links.
- **Online video clips and explanations:** Video clips of the CRI being administered, new interactives and other resources also are now available on the website *www.classroomreadinginventory.com.*
- **Favorite features streamlined and improved:** Updated word lists, correction of ambiguous items and improved formatting are additional improvements.
- **Web-based support and information from the authors:** The authors are pleased to provide through this edition updated formats and information at *www.classroomreadinginventory.com,* where you can access FAQs, case studies utilizing the CRI and an e-mail address for communications and questions. New additions include teaching types for professors, tutorials for communicating with parents and interviews with practitioners.

ACKNOWLEDGMENTS

We would like to thank the following reviewers whose comments helped form this revision.

Diane Brantley, California State University, San Bernardino

Cathleen Doheny, University of West Georgia

Marjaneh Gilpatrick, Grand Canyon University

Leigh Hall, University of North Carolina

Evan Ortlieb, Valdosta State University

Diane Pollard, Texas State University–San Marcos

Lynne Raiser, University of North Florida

Donita Massengill Shaw, University of Kansas

Nancy Walker, University of La Verne

Margaret Werts, Appalachian State University

INTRODUCTION

Overview of the CRI

The Classroom Reading Inventory (CRI) is a one-to-one assessment that enables the teacher to quickly diagnose a student's present ability to decode words both in isolation and in context, and to answer questions about the meaning. The CRI is designed to be used with all levels and ages of readers: elementary, middle school, high school and adult learners. The diagnostic subskills materials for high school and adult education students are available for download from the CRI website *www.classroomreadinginventory.com.*

The Classroom Reading Inventory brings to reading diagnosis the following benefits for both new teachers and the master teacher:

1. **Time efficacy:** After six to eight practice sessions, most teachers are able to complete a one-to-one CRI assessment within a 15-minute time frame.

2. **Clarity:** The teacher follows a step-by-step process that helps her make a valid and reliable interpretation of an individual's reading.

3. **Communication:** The CRI provides an assessment that is easy to understand by parents, tutors and other instructional support personnel.

4. **Multiple testing sessions:** The CRI provides multiple assessment forms, lists and passages so that individual progress can be measured over time.

5. **Value:** Teachers have unlimited permission granted by the publisher to reproduce inventory record forms. One CRI manual provides years of repeated use in a teacher's career.

The CRI has been in publication for more than forty years as a standard in the field of individual reading diagnosis. It is classified as an *informal reading inventory,* a literacy assessment based on sets of word lists and passages used to estimate students' oral and silent reading skills.

Informal reading inventories are also *criterion-referenced tests.* In the forty years since Nicholas Silveroli first introduced the CRI, the use of criterion-referenced tests has grown as policymakers seek greater documentation of what students actually know and can do. Criterion-based and outcome-based measures are now frequently required in federal and state accountability mandates.

As an informal reading inventory, the CRI allows the examiner to observe the student in the actual act of reading. Through this observation, the adult not only documents the level of reading mastery, but also the highly specific word recognition patterns and comprehension strengths and weaknesses required for personalized reading interventions and classroom lessons.

Such information comes from performance-based assessment. Observed behaviors, such as slow word-by-word reading rates or pattern of phonetic decoding difficulties, give powerful information for the correct instructional support that is not readily accessible on standardized group tests.

Purpose of the CRI in Educational Assessment

The CRI as a criterion test can be compared and contrasted to norm-based group tests. There are many norm-referenced reading assessments used to determine student reading achievement compared against those of national peers. This is a group testing model that can be termed *classification testing.*

A student assessed with a criterion-referenced assessment like that of the CRI is not compared to the performance of other students, as in norm-referenced testing. She is assessed against a standard of grade-level reading words and texts so that we can confirm her reading capacities regardless of the performance of any other boy or girl in the class, state or nation.

Differences Between Individual and Group Testing

The differences between individual and group testing can be illustrated by a brief description of the reading performances of two fifth-grade students, Eleni and Marco. Their norm-referenced test (NRT) results are:

> Eleni (10 years 9 months old): NRT 4.2 overall reading
> Marco (11 years 2 months old): NRT 4.2 overall reading

When we examine their NRT results, these two fifth-grade students appear to be about the same in age and overall reading achievement. However, data obtained from their individual CRIs indicate that there are significant *instructional* differences between these two students.

On the Graded Word Lists, Part 1 of the CRI, Eleni correctly pronounced all words at all grade levels, one through eight inclusive. It is evident that Eleni is well able to "sound out" or "decode" words. However, when Eleni read the Graded Paragraphs, Part 2, she was unable to answer many of the questions about these stories even at a first-grade-reader level of difficulty. Eleni is what is known as a *word caller.* That is, Eleni is quite proficient at decoding words, but she does not assign meaning to the words she decodes.

Marco, on the other hand, was able to answer questions about these same stories up to a fourth-grade-reader level of difficulty. However, his phonetic and structural analysis, or decoding, skills were inadequate for his level of development. Marco is what is known as a *context reader.* That is, even though his decoding skills are inadequate, he can usually answer questions based on the words he does decode and his background knowledge of the material.

The results obtained from an NRT concerning reading achievement tend to *classify* students as average, above average, or below average in terms of their reading achievement. While the results of an NRT may tell the teacher that a student is below average in reading, they cannot tell why the student is below average. These tests are not diagnostic. Therefore, as teachers, we need much more specific information about a student's decoding and comprehension skills if we are to be able to develop meaningful *independent* and *instructional* reading programs for every student.

An informal reading inventory does what an inventory is supposed to do—take stock. If a teacher knows what a student has in the way of phonetic and structural analysis skills, for example, then the teacher also knows what phonetic and structural analysis skills the student doesn't have. The same applies to the area of comprehension. The CRI is designed to provide teachers with just such specific and necessary diagnostic information.

Subskills Format

At the elementary and junior high/middle school levels, the Subskills Format enables the teacher to diagnose a student's ability to decode words (word recognition) both in isolation and in context and to answer questions (comprehension). In addition, the Subskills Format provides the teacher with a pretest and a posttest. The Subskills Format logically follows the type of reading instructional program being used in most elementary and junior high/middle schools.

At the high school and adult education levels, the Subskills Format enables the teacher to also diagnose a student's ability to decode words and to answer questions.

Reader Response Format

A number of classroom reading programs have shifted from a subskills instructional emphasis to a literacy emphasis. The Reader Response Format follows the type of literacy program that challenges students to use their inferential and critical reading and thinking abilities. The Reader Response Format provides the teacher with a pretest and a posttest for use with elementary and junior high/middle school students.

How Does the Subskills Format Differ from the Reader Response Format?

SUBSKILLS FORMAT: The Subskills Format enables the teacher to evaluate the student's ability to decode words in and out of context, and to evaluate the student's ability to answer factual/literal, vocabulary, and inference questions.

READER RESPONSE FORMAT: The Reader Response Format enables the teacher to evaluate various aspects of the student's comprehension ability by means of the following procedure. First, the student is asked to use the story title to *predict* what the story will be about. Second, the student is asked to *retell* the story or text with an emphasis on character(s), problem(s), and outcome(s)/solution(s).

SUBSKILLS FORMAT: Both formats use a *quantitative* scale for the evaluation of a student's reading ability. In the Subskills Format, if the student answers correctly four of the five questions, the student is considered to be *independent* in comprehension at that level. This format evaluates the student's ability to answer questions correctly.

READER RESPONSE FORMAT: In the Reader Response Format a number is assigned to the *quality* of the responses given by the student. For example, when the student is discussing character(s), the student is given zero credit for no response and three points if, in the teacher's judgment, the student's response is on target. The Reader Response Format is designed to enable the teacher to evaluate the student's ability to predict and retell narrative or expository texts.

Are There Other Differences?

SUBSKILLS FORMAT: Using the Subskills Format the teacher records correct and incorrect student responses and evaluates these responses to determine subskills needs in word recognition and comprehension.

READER RESPONSE FORMAT: The Reader Response Format requires the teacher to direct the student to make predictions about the story and to ask the student to retell what she can about the character(s), problem(s), and outcome(s)/solution(s) of the story. The teacher evaluates the student's thinking in terms of how the student makes inferences and summarizes information, to mention just two examples.

Are There Ways in Which These Formats Are Similar?

Both the Subskills Format and the Reader Response Format provide the teacher with authentic information. Both formats establish instructional reading levels.

Is the CRI Used with Groups or Individuals?

Within both formats, all six forms are to be used with individual students.

What Is Meant by Background Knowledge Assessment?

A student's background knowledge plays a crucial part in the reading comprehension process. Gunning (1998) writes, "Preparational strategies are those that a reader uses to prepare for reading. These include activating prior knowledge . . . and setting a goal for reading. [With] failure to activate prior knowledge, poor readers may not connect information in the text with what they already know."[1] It follows that the teacher should make a quick assessment of the student's background (prior) knowledge before the student is asked to read any narrative or expository material. Furthermore, the teacher should consider the amount of background (prior) knowledge when determining the levels.

What Readability Formula Was Used in the Development of the CRI?

For the Subskills Format Form A: Pretest and Posttest, and the Reader Response Format Form B: Pretest and Posttest, the Harris-Jacobson Wide Range Readability Formula[2] was used. This is also the case for the high school and adult Subskills Format.

How Were the Graded Paragraphs Developed and Accuracy Ensured?

All of the stories for the Graded Paragraphs are original stories written by the authors. All of the stories have been field-tested to ensure accurate level material has been written.

---

[1] Gunning, Thomas B. *Assessing and Correcting Reading and Writing Difficulties.* Allyn & Bacon, Boston, 1998, p. 314.
[2] Harris, Albert J., and Sipay, Edward R. *How to Increase Reading Ability,* 8th ed. Longman, New York, 1985, pp. 656–673.

CONDUCTING THE CLASSROOM READING INVENTORY

Preparing for the CRI Assessment

✓ Read all of the graded paragraphs. Some references may suit your student population better than others. Feel free to interchange the paragraphs contained in the Pre- and Posttests.

✓ Download or make a copy of the correct *Inventory Record for Teachers* scoring form. Forms A and B are in this manual and Form C can be downloaded from *www.classroomreadinginventory.com*. Forms A and B are suitable for kindergarten through 8th grade students and Form C is designed for high school and adult readers. In all, you have six forms available for multiple assessments:

SUBSKILL FORMAT

- Form A, Pretest (K–8th)
- Form A, Posttest (K–8th)
- Form C, Pretest (high school/adult)
- Form C, Posttest (high school/adult)

READER RESPONSE FORMAT

- Form B, Pretest (1st–8th)
- Form B, Posttest (1st–8th)

✓ You must have a basic understanding of the word recognition concepts listed on the Inventory Record Summary sheet, such as blends, digraphs and short vowels. See the Glossary of Basic Decoding Terminology on page 166.

✓ Note that the word count given in parentheses at the top of each paragraph in the Inventory Record for Teachers does not include the words in the title.

✓ Consider laminating the copies of the word lists and paragraphs from which the student reads. These are the ones in the back of the manual. Lamination keeps the pages in pristine condition so that you extend the life of your CRI edition.

Administering the CRI

✓ When administering the CRI, a right-handed teacher seems to have better control of the testing situation by placing the student to the left, thus avoiding the problem of having the inventory record forms between them.

✓ It is important to establish rapport with the student being tested. Avoid using words such as *test* or *test taking*. Instead, use words like *working with words, saying words for me, or talking about stories.*

✓ When you administer Part 2 (Graded Paragraphs), remove the student booklet before asking the questions on the comprehension check. Thus, the student is encouraged to recall information rather than merely locate answers in the material just read.

✓ When a student hesitates or cannot pronounce a word within five seconds in Part 2 (Graded Paragraphs), the teacher should *quickly* pronounce that word to maintain the flow of oral reading.

✓ Discontinue testing on Graded Paragraphs when the student reaches the Frustration Level in *either* word recognition or comprehension.

✓ You can use as silent reading selections any of the Graded Paragraphs, and Forms A, B, and C from the Subskills Format. Tell the student that he is to read the story silently and that you will still be asking him the questions. Before starting, do the Background Knowledge Assessment.

Scoring the CRI

The scoring guide on Form A, Pretest and Posttest, Part 2, of the Inventory Record for Teachers may cause some interpretation decisions. As an example, let's look at the scoring guide for the story "Our Bus Ride" from Form A, Part 2, Primer.

SIG WR Errors		COMP Errors	
IND (Independent)	0	IND (Independent)	0–1
INST (Instructional)	3	INST (Instructional)	1½–2
FRUST (Frustration)	6+	FRUST (Frustration)	2½+

Should IND or INST be circled if a student makes one or two significant word recognition errors? It is the authors' opinion that (a) if the student's comprehension is at the independent level, select the independent level for word recognition; (b) if in doubt, select the lowest level. This practice is referred to as *undercutting*. If the teacher undercuts or underestimates the student's instructional level, the chances of success at the initial point of instruction increase.

At any rate, it is the teacher who makes the decision. To help you make this decision, take into account those *qualitative* features such as, was it a fluent and expressive reading, or was it word-by-word? When you take into account *qualitative* features there will be less confusion as to which level to indicate. Remember: It is you the teacher who makes the decision—not the test.

USING THE CRI:
SPECIFIC INSTRUCTIONS

For Administering the Subskills Format
Form A: Pretest and Form A: Posttest

PART 1—Graded Word Lists: Subskills Format

Purposes:
1. To identify specific word recognition errors.
2. To estimate the starting level at which the student begins reading the Graded Paragraphs in Part 2.

Procedure:
Always begin Part 1 Graded Word Lists at the Preprimer (PP) level. Present the Graded Word Lists to the student and say:

> "I have some words on these lists, and I want you to say them out loud for me. If you come to a word you don't know, it's OK to say 'I don't know.' Just do the best you can."

Discontinue at the level at which the student mispronounces or indicates she does not know five of the twenty words at a particular grade level (75 percent). Each correct response is worth five points.

As the student pronounces the words at each level, the teacher should record all word responses on the Inventory Record for Teachers.[1] Self-corrected errors are counted as acceptable responses in Part 1. These recorded word responses may be analyzed later to determine specific word recognition needs.

How to Record Student Responses to the Graded Word Lists

1. came   ✓   The checkmark (✓) means the student decoded the word *came* correctly.
2. liberty   *library*   The student decoded the word *liberty* as *library*.
3. stood   *P*   The *P* means the student did not respond to the word *stood* and the teacher pronounced it to maintain an even flow.
4. car   +/*can*   Initially, the student decoded *car* as *can* but quickly corrected the error. This is a self-corrected error as indicated by the + sign.
5. turkeys   (S)   The (S) means the student left off the *s* in *turkeys,* and pronounced it as *turkey.* Anything circled on the CRI indicates where something has been omitted.
6. chase   *d*   The *d* not encircled means the student added a *d* to the word *chase* and pronounced it as *chased.* The use of an encircled omitted ending, or an uncircled added word ending, enables the teacher to speed up the recording process.
7. guides   *gēds*   The student decoded the word *guides* by using a nonsense word. When this happens, record a phonetic approximation of the nonsense word given. In this example, the student said *gēds.*

---

[1] The Inventory Record for Teachers is a separate record form printed on standard 8 1/2 × 11 paper. *Note:* Teachers may download from the Inventory Record for Teachers at *www.classroomreadinginventory.com.*

PART 2—Graded Paragraphs: Subskills Format

Purposes:
1. To estimate the student's independent and instructional levels. Also, to identify the student's frustration level and, if necessary, the student's listening capacity level.
2. To identify significant word recognition errors made during oral reading and to determine the extent to which the student actually comprehends what he reads.

Procedure:
Present the Graded Paragraphs starting at the highest level at which the student decoded correctly all twenty words on the Graded Word Lists, Part 1, and say:

> "I have some stories here that I want you to read out loud to me. After you finish
> a story, I will ask you some questions about what you read."

At this point introduce each story to be read by completing the Background Knowledge Assessment (e.g., say "This story is about puppies. What can you tell me about puppies?").

Levels

What follows is a brief explanation of each of the four *levels* that apply to Subskills Format Form A. These four levels are referred to as Independent (IND), Instructional (INST), Frustration (FRUST), and Listening Capacity (LC).

Independent Level

The independent level is defined as adequate functioning in reading with no help from the teacher. Adequate functioning means 99 percent accuracy in word recognition and with 90 percent comprehension or better.[2] The teacher will use the independent level estimate in selecting supplementary reading material and the library and trade books students can read comfortably on their own. Since this is the type of reading students will be doing for personal recreation and information, it is important that the students be given reading material from which they can extract content without the hazards of unfamiliar words and concepts.

Instructional Level

As the selections become more difficult, the student will reach a level at which she can read with at least 95 percent accuracy in word recognition and with 75 percent comprehension or better. At this level the student needs the teacher's help. This is the student's instructional level, useful in determining the level of textbook that can be read with some teacher guidance.

Frustration Level

When the student reads a selection that is beyond the recommended instructional level, the teacher may well observe symptoms of frustration such as anxiety, tension, excessive finger-pointing, and slow, halting, word-by-word reading. Word recognition accuracy drops to 90 percent or lower. Comprehension may be extremely poor, with 50 percent or lower accuracy. Usually most of the concepts and questions are inaccurately discussed by the student. This represents a level that should be avoided when textbooks and supplementary reading material are being selected.

---

[2] The actual number of significant word recognition and comprehension errors permissible at each grade level can be found in the separate Inventory Record for Teachers.

Listening Capacity Level

The listening capacity level is defined as adequate understanding of material that is read to the student by the examiner. Listening capacity is assessed to determine whether the student can understand and discuss what he listened to at levels beyond the frustration level. It is assumed that the reading skills might be improved through further instruction, at least to the listening capacity level. A score of 70 percent or better is an indication of adequate understanding.

Not all students are administered the listening capacity assessment. For when, and when not, to use the listening capacity assessment see the sample CRI records on p. 19.

When the teacher makes a decision that a student has reached the frustration level in either word recognition and/or comprehension, this part of the testing is concluded. The teacher then decides whether to go to the listening capacity format. To see how one teacher makes this decision, check the sample CRI records on p. 29.

GENERAL INTRODUCTION TO MISCUE ANALYSIS

Recording Word Recognition Errors

There was a time when it was assumed that all word recognition errors were of equal significance: an error is an error is an error. As such, the teacher was asked merely to *quantify,* or count, all word recognition errors and regard them as equal. The CRI requires the teacher to count errors (quantitative) and also to reflect about what the student actually is doing as she makes the error (qualitative); that is, what caused the student to make the error?

In general, a word recognition error should be judged as *significant* (high-weighted) if the error impacts or interferes with the student's fluency or thought process. *Insignificant* (low-weighted) word recognition errors are minor alterations and do not interfere with student fluency or cognition; for example, the student substitutes *a* for *the* before a noun or infrequently omits or adds a word ending. These are very common miscues.

The following examples are designed to enable teachers to make qualitative judgments of significant and insignificant word recognition errors. It is impossible, however, to account for all possibilities. With this in mind, teachers are advised to use this information as a guide to establish their own criteria for developing a qualitative mind-set by which to determine whether a word recognition error is significant or insignificant. The more a teacher thinks about what caused an error, the better that teacher will be able to understand the decoding process.

Significant and Insignificant Word Recognition Errors

The following are examples of common word recognition error types.

- **Example:** The turkey is a silly bird.
  (P above "turkey")

The student does not recognize a word and *needs teacher assistance.* This is symbolized by placing a *P* (for *pronounced*) over the word not recognized. This is always regarded as a significant error.

- **Example:** The cat chased the birds. OR It was a very hot day.

The student *omits* a word or part of a word. This is symbolized by drawing a circle around the omitted word or word part. Infrequent omissions are considered insignificant word recognition errors. Frequent omissions, however, are significant. There is no definite number that indicates infrequent/frequent omissions. Only you the teacher, as you listen to the student read, can determine what is infrequent/frequent. The teacher is the decision maker.

- **Example:**   *Significant:*   Baby birds like to eat seeds and grain.
  (grin above "grain")

  Insignificant: He went to the store. OR
  (a above "the")

  The children were lost in the forest.
  (woods above "forest")

The student *substitutes* a word for the word as given. This is symbolized by writing the word substituted above the word as given. This type of error is judged to be significant if it impacts or interferes with fluency or cognition. However, it may also be judged as insignificant if it does not interfere with fluency or cognition.

- **Example:** *Significant:*
  don't
  The trees ^ look small.

  Insignificant:
  so
  The trees look ^ small.

The student *inserts* a word into the sentence. This is symbolized by the use of a caret (^) with the inserted word above the caret. Insertions are usually regarded as insignificant word recognition errors because they tend to embellish what the student is reading. However, if the insertion changes the meaning of what is being read, it should be judged as significant.

- **Example:** *Significant:*
  They were bound ⌒ for the salt springs ⌒ near the mountains.

  Insignificant:
  The crowd ⌒ at the rodeo stood up.

The student repeats a word or words. This is symbolized by drawing an arc over the repeated word(s). Repetitions are usually considered to be insignificant errors if they are infrequent. However, excessive repetitions suggest the need for more reading practice, and they should be judged as significant. What is infrequent/excessive is the teacher's decision.

As teachers become accustomed to thinking qualitatively about why students make the errors they do, they will become more sensitive to a qualitative analysis of word recognition errors. As such, teachers will begin to better understand the decoding process and what mediates error behavior. The following are examples of enhanced sensitivity on the part of teachers regarding qualitative analysis.

- **Example:** The bird̶s̶ ̶a̶r̶e̶ singing.
  is

This is an example of omission and word substitution. The first error, omitted *s*, caused the second error, substituting *is* for *are*. If the student did not substitute *is* for *are,* language dissonance would occur.

- **Example:** How high w̶e̶ ̶a̶r̶e̶?
  are we

This shows two word substitution errors of a reversal word order. These errors were caused by the first word *How. How,* at the beginning of a sentence, usually signals to the reader that it will be a question. This is just what the reader did: anticipated a question and made it into a question. This counts as only one error.

- **Example:** I̶t̶ ̶i̶s̶ a work car.
  It's

Here two words are contracted because it is more natural to say *it's* than *it is.* Remember, it's not a case of how many errors (quantitative) but, rather, what causes the errors (qualitative). The more you become accustomed to thinking about errors, the better you will be able to understand the decoding process.

As the authors indicated in the introduction to this section, it is impossible to account for all possible miscues. Some miscues are errors of anticipation. For example, a student is reading a sentence and he senses that a noun is coming up. The student also knows that before that noun there will be either the definite article *the,* or the indefinite article *a.* Sensing the approach of the noun, the student in this example anticipates the definite article *the.* Even if it turns out that the article is the indefinite *a,* the student is likely to read *the,* for this is what he anticipated. The reverse is also true.

Language or regional dialect differences can also be miscues and should not be regarded as decoding errors, but as language differences. For example, a student comes to the word *fingers* on the Graded Word Lists. She read *fingers* as *fangers.* How can we be sure, then, that this is due to language differences and not a decoding error? Easy; the teacher asks, "what are *fangers?*" The student holds up a hand and says, "*these are my fangers.*" Dialect, not decoding!

Students whose first language is Spanish typically have difficulty with the way in English the *ch* and *sh* sounds are articulated. As such, the English as a second language (ESL) student may decode the word *chair* as *share.* Language difficulty, not decoding!

Marking Word Recognition Errors on Graded Paragraphs

- **Example:** Elephants are unusual animals.
  (P above "unusual")

Student does not recognize a word. Teacher pronounces the word for the student and marks it with a *P.*

- **Example:** We are ~~ready~~ to go now.
  (riding above "ready")

Student substitutes a word for the word as given. Teacher writes the substituted word above the given word.

- **Example:** After week⑤ of hunting . . .

- **Example:** It was a ⟨good⟩ day for a ride.

Student omits a word(s) or a word part. Teacher draws a circle around the omitted word(s) or word part.

- **Example:** Mike is John's ^ friend.
  (best above caret)

Student inserts a word into the body of a sentence. Teacher uses a caret to show where the word was inserted.

- **Example:** It was a good day for a ride.
  (arc over "It was" and over "a ride")

Student repeats a word(s). Teacher draws an arc over the repeated word(s).

Evaluating Comprehension Responses

After each graded paragraph, the student is asked to answer questions. The separate Inventory Record for Teachers labels questions as follows:

(F) Factual or Literal
(I) Inference
(V) Vocabulary

Suggested answers are listed after each question. However, these answers are to be read as guides or probable answers. The teacher must judge the adequacy of each response made by the student. In most cases it is helpful to record student responses if they differ from the listed suggested responses.

Scoring Guide

What follows is a scoring guide for the story "Given the Opportunity".

Scoring Guide	Fifth		
SIG WR Errors		**COMP Errors**	
IND	2	IND	0–1
INST	8	INST	1 ½–2
FRUST		FRUST	2 ½+

The scoring guide for all levels in Part 2 Graded Paragraphs uses error limits for the reader—in other words, Independent (IND), Instructional (INST) and Frustration (FRUST) reading levels.

As such, the guide suggests that when a student reads "Given the Opportunity" and makes two Significant (SIG) Word Recognition (WR) errors, the student is able to Independently (IND) decode typical fifth-grade words. Eight Significant (SIG) errors at this level suggest an Instructional (INST) level. Seventeen Significant Word Recognition errors suggest that the student is Frustrated (FRUST) in Word Recognition at this level.[3] The same scoring rationale should be applied to the comprehension portion of the guide.

This guide is for the teacher to use in determining *realistic* independent and instructional levels. What if the student were to make three Significant Word Recognition errors? Or four? Does this indicate Independent or Instructional in decoding? The student's responses to words and questions must be evaluated by the teacher. Questions like these will be addressed in much greater depth in the next section: CRI INTERPRETATION. The scoring guide is just that—a guide. The teacher, not the guide, makes the final diagnosis.

Quick Reference for Abbreviations

- SIG WR = Significant Word Recognition

- COMP = Comprehension

- IND = Independent Level

- INST = Instructional Level

- FRUST = Frustration Level

- CRI = Classroom Reading Inventory

- (F) = Factual or Literal

- (I) = Inference

- (V) = Vocabulary

---

[3] See pages 8–9 for a discussion of these levels.

Summary of Specific Instructions

Step 1   Establish rapport. Don't be in a hurry to begin testing. Put the student at ease. Make her feel comfortable.

Step 2   Administer Part 1 Graded Word Lists. Always begin testing at the Preprimer level.

Step 3   Administer Part 2 Graded Paragraphs. Begin at the highest level at which the student knew all twenty words in Part 1, Graded Word Lists.

Step 4   Background Knowledge Assessment. Before starting a graded paragraph, engage the student in a brief discussion about the story to be read. Attempt to uncover what the student knows about the topic, and try to get the student to make predictions about the story. If the student has some background knowledge, rate the student as *adequate*. If little or no background knowledge is evident, mark as *inadequate*.

Step 5   Graded Paragraphs. Have the student read the selection out loud. Make certain that the student understands that he will be asked to answer questions after each selection.

Step 6   Ask the questions, and be sure to record the student's responses if they differ from suggested responses.

Step 7   On the Graded Paragraphs, if the student reaches the frustration level in either word recognition or comprehension, or both, stop at that level.

Step 8   Complete the Inventory Record, and use the information garnered from the Graded Word Lists and the Graded Paragraphs to determine the estimated levels.

Step 9   Remember! It is the teacher that makes the final diagnosis (qualitative), not the number of errors recorded (quantitative).

CRI SCORING AND INTERPRETATION

Subskills Format
Form A: Pretest and Form A: Posttest

The CRI is designed to provide the teacher with a realistic estimate of the student's independent, instructional, frustration, and listening capacity levels in reading. However, merely identifying various reading levels is only slightly better than classifying the student on the basis of a norm-referenced test score.

The CRI is much more effective when the teacher is able to pinpoint consistent errors in word recognition or comprehension, or both. The CRI should enable the teacher to answer these specific questions.

- What is inhibiting fluent reading with comprehension? Is my student having difficulty recognizing the words (decoding function), or understanding the content (meaning function), or both?
- If the student's difficulty is in the area of word recognition, are there problems with consonants, vowels, or structure/syllables?
- If the student's difficulty is comprehension, are the problems with factual/literal questions, vocabulary questions, or inferential questions?
- Is the student a word caller, or a context reader?
- Does the student appear to have other needs? Does it appear that he needs glasses? Does the student appear to be anxious or withdrawn while reading aloud? Are high-interest/easy reading materials needed?

The following are case studies of the administration of the Classroom Reading Inventory. You can read these case studies here in the manual, or see them modeled by Dr. Wheelock with actual children playing the parts of Deon and Anna on the website *www.classroomreadinginventory.com*.

The website also has additional case studies and reporting formats of clinical assessments for your review. Please note that these examples include some stories in the 12th edition as well as words and stories from previous editions.

DEMONSTRATION OF THE CRI

Sample CRI Record—Deon

Deon is a fourth-grade student who is 9 years, 6 months old. His IQ, as measured by the Wechsler Intelligence Scale for Children–III, is in the average range. His grade equivalency in reading is 2.8, as measured by a group reading achievement test.

The score on the group reading achievement test is an indication that Deon's reading is below average for his grade level. The indication of below average reading, however, does not explain *why* Deon's reading is below average.

In order to determine why Deon's reading is not at grade level, Deon's teacher, Doris Cadd, administered Form A: Pretest of the CRI to Deon. His Inventory Record and Summary Sheet follow on pages 19 to 20.

Getting Started—Graded Word Lists:

Ms. Cadd: Deon, I have some words on these lists, and I want you to say them out loud for me. If you come to a word you don't know, it's OK to say "I don't know." Just do the best you can.

Ms. Cadd then places the Form A: Pretest Preprimer-Primer (PP-P) Graded Word Lists in front of Deon, and pointing to the first word *this* on the preprimer list says, "OK, start here."

As Deon decodes the words on these lists, Ms. Cadd records his responses in the Inventory Record for Teachers, Form A. This procedure is followed with successive Graded Word Lists until the student misses five or more words in any column, at which point this part of the testing is stopped.

Ms. Cadd then moves on to the Graded Paragraphs.

Form A: Pretest Inventory Record
Summary Sheet

Student's Name: _Deon R._ **Grade:** _4_ **Age:** _9-6_
year, months

Date: _10/17/10_ **School:** _Robinson E.S._   **Administered by:** _Doris Cadd_

Part 1 — Word Lists			Part 2 — Graded Paragraphs			

Part 1 — Word Lists

Grade Level	Percentage of Words Correct	Word Recognition Errors
PP	_100%_	**Consonants**
P	_90%_	____ consonants / ✓ blends
1	_80%_	____ digraphs / ✓ endings
2	_70%_	____ compounds / ____ contractions
3	___ %	**Vowels**
4	___ %	____ long / ✓ short
5	___ %	____ long/short oo / ✓ vowel + r
6	___ %	____ diphthong / ✓ vowel comb.
7	___ %	____ a + l or w
8	___ %	**Syllable** ✓ visual patterns / ✓ prefix / ✓ suffix

Word Recognition Reinforcement and Vocabulary Development

Part 2 — Graded Paragraphs

	SIG WR	COMP	LC
PP	IND	IND	
P	INST	IND	
1	INST	IND	
2	FRUST	IND	
3			100%
4			80%
5			40%
6			
7			
8			

Estimated Levels

	Grade
Independent	PP
Instructional	P–1 (range)
Frustration	2
Listening Capacity	4

Comp Errors
____ Factual (F)
____ Inference (I)
____ Vocabulary (V)
____ "Word Caller"
     (A student who reads without associating meaning)
____ Poor Memory

Summary of Specific Needs:

Problems with phonetic and structural analysis. Needs help with short vowel sounds and irregular vowel combinations.

Form A: Pretest   Part 1   Graded Word Lists

PP		P		1		2	
1. this	✓	1. came	✓	1. new	_now_	1. birthday	✓
2. her	✓	2. day	✓	2. leg	✓	2. free	✓
3. about	✓	3. big	✓	3. feet	✓	3. isn't	✓
4. to	✓	4. house	✓	4. hear	_her_	4. beautiful	_boo-ful_
5. are	✓	5. after	✓	5. food	✓	5. job	✓
6. you	✓	6. how	✓	6. learn	✓	6. elephant	_P_
7. he	✓	7. put	✓	7. hat	✓	7. cowboy	✓
8. all	✓	8. other	_P_	8. ice	✓	8. branch	_beach_
9. like	✓	9. went	_want_	9. letter	✓	9. asleep	✓
10. could	✓	10. just	✓	10. green	✓	10. mice	✓
11. my	✓	11. play	✓	11. outside	✓	11. corn	✓
12. said	✓	12. many	✓	12. happy	✓	12. baseball	✓
13. was	✓	13. trees	✓	13. less	✓	13. garden	_grāden_
14. look	✓	14. boy	✓	14. drop	✓	14. hall	✓
15. go	✓	15. good	✓	15. stopping	(_ing_)	15. pet	✓
16. down	✓	16. girl	✓	16. grass	✓	16. blows	(_s_)
17. with	✓	17. see	✓	17. street	✓	17. gray	✓
18. what	✓	18. something	✓	18. page	✓	18. law	✓
19. been	✓	19. little	✓	19. ever	_even_	19. bat	✓
20. on	✓	20. saw	✓	20. let's	✓	20. guess	_gross_
	_100%_		_90%_		_80%_		_70%_

Teacher note: If the child misses five words in any column—stop Part 1. Begin Graded Paragraphs, Part 2 (Form A: Pretest), at the highest level in which the child recognized all 20 words. Each correct response equals 5%.

Scoring and Interpretation for Sample CRI—Deon

Part 1 Graded Words Lists—Scoring

- At the Preprimer (PP) level, Deon decoded all twenty words correctly. Score = 100%.

- At the Primer (P) level, Deon did not recognize word number 8 *other*. Therefore, Ms. Cadd pronounced the word *other* for Deon to maintain the flow and marked a *P* for *Pronounced*. Deon decoded *want* as *went*, and Ms. Cadd wrote *want* alongside the stimulus word *went*. Score = 90%.

- At Level 1 (first grade), Deon said *now* for *new*, *her* for *hear*, omitted the *ing* ending on *stopping*, and said *even* for *ever*. Score = 80%.

- At Level 2 (second grade), Deon decoded *beautiful* with a nonsense word *boo-ful*. He failed to decode *elephant*, and Ms. Cadd pronounced it for him. Deon said *beach* for *branch*, decoded *garden* with a nonsense word *grāden*, omitted the *s* ending of the word *blows*, and said *gross* for *guess*. Score = 70%.

- Part 1 is now completed because Deon scored at 75% or below.

Part 1 Graded Word Lists—Interpretation

- For a fourth grader, Deon's phonetic and structural analysis skills are inadequate for his level of development. He appears to have particular difficulty with short vowel sounds and irregular vowel combinations such as *r* affected vowels and vowel digraphs. His basic sight word vocabulary also appears to be lacking.

- Let us now proceed to Part 2 Graded Paragraphs. Ms. Cadd will start Deon at the Preprimer (PP) level as that's the level where Deon had all twenty words decoded correctly on Part 1 Graded Word Lists. Watch Dr. Wheelock demonstrate in the video at the website *www.classroomreadinginventory.com*.

Getting Started—Graded Paragraphs:

Ms. Cadd: Deon, on this part I have some stories that I want you to read out loud to me. After you finish a story, I will ask you some questions about what you read.

At this point, Ms. Cadd introduces the Preprimer story "The Play Car" and completes the Background Knowledge Assessment by saying, "This story is about two children and a play car. Tell me what you think the children are doing."

Once the Background Knowledge Assessment has been completed, Ms. Cadd says, "Fine, Deon. Now, read this story out loud to me. It is called "The Play Car."

When Deon finishes reading "The Play Car," Ms. Cadd removes the story from view and asks Deon the five questions.

This procedure is followed with successive stories until the student reaches the Frustration Level in word recognition and/or comprehension.

Form A: Pretest   Part 2/Level PP (38 Words)

Background Knowledge Assessment: This story is about two children and a play car. Tell me what you think the children are doing.

Adequate [✓]   Inadequate [ ]

THE PLAY CAR

Tom has a play car.

His play car is red.

"See my play car," said Tom.

"It can go fast."

Ann said, "It's a big car."

"I like your car."

"Good," said Tom.

"Would you like a ride?"
                  to

Comprehension Check

(F) 1. ___✓___ What are the names of the boy and girl in this story?
(Tom and Ann)

(F) 2. ___✓___ What were they talking about?
(The play car)

(F) 3. ___✓___ Who owns the play car?
(Tom)

(F) 4. ___✓___ What color is the car?
(Red)

(I) 5. ___✓___ What do you think Tom likes about the car?
(It is big, fast)

Scoring Guide   Preprimer

SIG WR Errors		**COMP Errors**	
(IND)	0	(IND)	0–1
INST	2	INST	$1\frac{1}{2}$–2
FRUST	4+	FRUST	$2\frac{1}{2}$+

Background Knowledge Assessment: Has your class ever taken a field trip? Tell me about a field trip.

Adequate [✓]   Inadequate [ ]

OUR BUS RIDE

The children were all talking.

"No more talking, children," said Mrs. Brown.

"It is time for our trip."

"It is time to go to the farm."

Mrs. Brown said, "Get in the bus."

"Please do not push anyone."

riding
"We are ready to go now."

P
The children climbed into the bus.

Away went the bus.

the
It was a good day for a trip.

Comprehension Check

(F) 1. __✓__ Where are they going?
(Farm)

(F) 2. __✓__ How are they going?
(By bus)

(I) 3. __✓__ Who do you think
Mrs. Brown is?
(Teacher, bus driver, a parent)

(F) 4. __✓__ How did the children know
that it was time for the bus to
leave?
(Mrs. Brown said, "We are
ready to go now.") *Teacher told*
them

(I) 5. __✓__ Why do you think
Mrs. Brown asked the children
not to push anyone?
(Prevent accidents, any other
reasonable answer)

Scoring Guide   Primer

SIG WR Errors   **COMP Errors**

IND	0	IND	0–1
INST	3	INST	$1\frac{1}{2}$–2
FRUST	6+	FRUST	$2\frac{1}{2}$+

Form A: Pretest   Part 2/Level 1 (71 Words)

Background Knowledge Assessment: This story is about puppies. What can you tell me about puppies?

Adequate [✓]   Inadequate [　]

MARIA'S PUPPIES

Maria has two puppies.

She thinks that puppies are fun to ~~watch~~. *wash*

The puppies' names are *Sissy* and *Sassy*.

Puppies are ~~born~~ with their eyes closed. *brown*

Their ears are closed, too.

This is why they use their smell and touch.

After two weeks, puppies begin to open their eyes and ears.

Most puppies can bark after four weeks.

Maria knows that *Sissy* and *Sassy* will grow up ~~to~~ be good pets. *and*

.

Comprehension Check

(F) 1. ___✓___   How many puppies does Maria have?
(Two)

(F) 2. __1/2__   What are the puppies' names?
(Sissy and Sassy)   *Sissy and Sally*

(I) 3. ___✓___   Why do you think that Maria thinks puppies are fun to watch?
(Any reasonable answer; e.g., they jump, roll around, chase their tails)

(F) 4. ___✓___   What can puppies do after four weeks?
(Bark)

(F) 5. ___✓___   At birth, puppies must use their sense of smell and touch. Why?
(Eyes or ears closed)

Scoring Guide   First

SIG WR Errors		COMP Errors	
~~IND~~	0	(IND)	0–1
(INST)	3	INST	$1\frac{1}{2}$–2
~~FRUST~~	6+	FRUST	$2\frac{1}{2}$+

Form A: Pretest   Part 2/Level 2 (76 Words)

Background Knowledge Assessment: What kinds of shows do you like to watch on TV?

Adequate [✓]   Inadequate [ ]

HOMEWORK FIRST

Marco and his sister Teresa love to ~~watch~~ *wash* TV.

The shows ~~they~~ *that* like best are cartoons. *P*

Every day ~~after~~ *for* school they go out(side) to play.

Soon, Mother calls (to) them to come in.

"It's time to do your homework," she says. *P*

"When you finish *flash* your homework you can

watch your cartoons," Mother promises. *P*

"Remember! Homework first." *P*

Marco and Teresa are happy with this.

They do their homework.

Now they are ready to watch ~~their~~ *the* cartoon

shows.

Comprehension Check

(F) 1. ____✓____ What do Marco and Teresa do first when they come home? (They go outside and play)

(F) 2. ____✓____ What did their mother promise them? (When they finish their homework they can watch cartoons [TV])

(V) 3. ____DK____ What does *promise* mean? (To do what you say you will do; or any other reasonable answer)

(F) 4. ____✓____ What kinds of shows do Marco and Teresa like to watch the most? (Cartoons)

(I) 5. ____✓____ Other than cartoons, what shows do you think Marco and Teresa watch? (Any reasonable answer; e.g., movies, MTV, sports)

Scoring Guide   Second

SIG WR Errors

IND	2
INST	4
(FRUST)	8+

COMP Errors

(IND)	0–1
INST	$1\frac{1}{2}$–2
FRUST	$2\frac{1}{2}$+

Background Knowledge Assessment: Have you ever been to Chicago? What do you know about Chicago?

Adequate [✓]   Inadequate [ ]

THE GREAT CHICAGO FIRE

It was early October of 1871. It was very dry in Chicago. Hardly any rain had fallen between July and October. Then on the evening of October 8, 1871, a fire started in the southwest side of the city.

It is believed the fire started in a barn owned by Mrs. Patrick O'Leary. A cow kicked over a lantern in the barn. There were strong winds that night. Flames raced north and east through the city. Many families fled north to Lincoln Park. Many other families raced into the cold waters of Lake Michigan. The fire wiped out the downtown area and most north side homes killing many people.

Chicago rose from the ruins of the fire to become one of the world's greatest cities.

Comprehension Check

(F) 1. ___✓___ How did the Chicago Fire start? (A cow kicked over a lantern in Mrs. O'Leary's barn)

(F) 2. ___✓___ Why was it so dry in Chicago when the fire started? (Very little rain had fallen that summer)

(V) 3. ___✓___ What is a *lantern*? (Like a lamp)

(I) 4. ___✓___ Why do you think many families fled to Lincoln Park? (Very little to burn in a park, or any other reasonable answer)

(F) 5. ___✓___ What month was it when the fire started? (October)

100%

Scoring Guide   Third

SIG WR Errors		COMP Errors	
IND	2	IND	0–1
INST	7	INST	$1^1/_2$–2
FRUST	14	FRUST	$2^1/_2$ +

Form A: Pretest **Part 2/Level 4 (166 Words)**

Background Knowledge Assessment: Rosa Parks played a very important part in the Civil Rights Movement. What can you tell me about Rosa Parks or the Civil Rights Movement?

Adequate [✓]   Inadequate [ ]

TIRED OF GIVING IN

It was warm that December afternoon in Montgomery, Alabama. Rosa Parks was waiting for her city bus. She was tired from a long day of work—sewing.

When her bus came, Rosa took an empty seat in the "colored" section. In 1955, blacks could not sit in the front of the bus. However, they had to give up their seats in the middle to any white left standing.

Soon the front of the bus filled up. The white driver ordered Rosa to give up her seat to a white man. She didn't move. The driver called the police. Rosa was arrested.

Almost all of Montgomery's blacks, and some whites, staged a year-long boycott of the bus system to protest Rosa's arrest. The boycott was led by Martin Luther King, Jr. It ended when the Supreme Court ruled all bus segregation illegal.

Years later, Rosa Parks said, "I didn't give up my seat because I was tired. The only tired I was, was tired of giving in."

Comprehension Check

(F) 1. ___✓___ Why was Rosa Parks arrested?
(She wouldn't give up her seat)

(V) 2. ___✓___ What does the word *illegal* mean?
(Against the law, not legal)

(F) 3. ___✓___ Who led the boycott of the bus system?
(Martin Luther King, Jr.)

(I) 4. __DK__ What do you think Rosa Parks meant when she said, "I was tired of giving in"?
(Any reasonable answer; e.g., she was tired of doing something that was not fair)

(I) 5. ___✓___ Where do you think Rosa was going when she got on the bus?
(Any reasonable answer; e.g., home, to visit a friend)

80%

Scoring Guide   Fourth

SIG WR Errors		COMP Errors	
IND	3	IND	0–1
INST	8	INST	$1^1/_2$–2
FRUST	16	FRUST	$2^1/_2$ +

Background Knowledge Assessment: What do you know about pirates?

Adequate [✓] Inadequate [ ]

PIRATES!

Pirates were people who attacked and robbed ships. They raided towns like Charleston, South Carolina. Most people who became pirates hoped to get rich. Most pirates were men. A few women became pirates, too.

Movies have given us the idea that pirates led exciting lives. In real life, however, most pirates led miserable lives. Many pirates died of wounds or disease. Many were captured and hanged.

In the early 1700s, pirates sailed along the coast of South Carolina. They robbed ships sailing to or from Charleston. There were so many pirates around Charleston that few ships were safe.

One of these pirates was Stede Bonnet. Bonnet was very mean. He was the first pirate to make people "walk the plank."

William Rhett set out to capture Bonnet. He did, and took Bonnet and his crew to Charleston. All of Bonnet's crew were hanged. Just before Bonnet was to be hanged, a friend took him some women's clothes. Dressed as a woman, Bonnet was able to escape. Rhett went after him again. Bonnet was brought back to Charleston and hanged.

Pirates are gone now, but their stories live on.

Comprehension Check

(F) 1. ___—___   How did Bonnet escape from jail? *He ran away* (He dressed as a woman)

(F) 2. ___✓___   What happened to Bonnet? (He was hanged)

(I) 3. ___✓___   Why do you think some women became pirates? (Any reasonable answer; e.g., they wanted to get rich; they were married to pirates; they thought it would be exciting)

(V) 4. ___DK___   What does the word *coast* mean in this story? (Where the land meets the sea; the beach)

(I) 5. ___DK___   What do you think *walk the plank* means? (The pirates forced people to walk on a board until they fell overboard)

40%

Scoring Guide   Fifth

SIG WR Errors		COMP Errors	
IND	2	IND	0–1
INST	8	INST	$1\frac{1}{2}$–2
FRUST	17+	FRUST	$2\frac{1}{2}$+

Scoring and Interpretation for Sample CRI—Deon

Part 2 Graded Paragraphs—Scoring

Deon read aloud the Preprimer story. Because his only word recognition error (Deon said *to* for *a*) is a low-weighted (insignificant) error, Deon is considered to be independent for word recognition. Deon answered all of the questions correctly, so he is judged to be independent in comprehension.

In reading the Primer story, Deon made two significant word recognition errors. He said *riding* for *ready,* and Ms. Cadd had to pronounce *climbed* for him. In addition, there was one insignificant word recognition error. Deon said *the* for *a.* He is considered to be instructional for word recognition. Deon answered all of the questions correctly, so he is judged to be independent in comprehension.

Deon read the First Grade story and made two significant word recognition errors. He said *wash* for *watch,* and *brown* for *born.* Deon also made one insignificant word recognition error when he said *and* for *to.* Notice that in so doing he did not affect the meaning of the sentence. Deon answered four of the five questions correctly, and for one question he was given one-half credit because he miscalled one of the puppies' names. Deon is independent in comprehension.

From the number of significant word recognition errors Deon made with the Second Grade story, it is clear that he has reached frustration level with word recognition. His comprehension, however, continues to be at an independent level. At this point further oral reading of the graded paragraphs is discontinued.

Because Deon cannot decode successfully beyond a second-grade level, Ms. Cadd has decided to use the Listening Capacity Format in order to judge Deon's level of comprehension. Even with all of the decoding errors Deon made at the second-grade level, his comprehension is at the independent level.

Ms. Cadd decides to begin the Listening Capacity Format at the next highest level, the third-grade level.

Ms. Cadd: Deon, for these next stories, I will read the story out loud to you. You can follow the story as I read it. I will still ask you the questions at the end of the story. Be sure to pay close attention!

Ms. Cadd then places the Form A: Pretest Third Grade story, "Pony Express," in front of Deon while she reads the story to Deon from her copy. Upon completing the story, Ms. Cadd removes Deon's copy from view, and asks him the five questions.

This procedure is followed with successive stories until the student's level of comprehension falls below 70% on any given story.

Do not use the Scoring Guide for the Listening Capacity Format. Go to a numerical marking system instead. For example, a correct answer is worth 20 points, a one-half credit is worth 10 points, and no points for a wrong answer. Record the score after the last question.

With the Third Grade story comprehension was 100%, and 80% with the Fourth Grade story. With the Fifth Grade story comprehension dropped to 40%, which indicates inadequate comprehension at this level. No further testing of Deon is done.

Part 2 Graded Paragraphs—Interpretation

The results of Deon's testing on the CRI clearly indicate a problem with decoding. His phonetic and structural analysis skills are inadequate for his level of development. His comprehension, however, of stories he read, and stories read to him, was very good through a fourth-grade-reader level of difficulty. Deon is a **context reader.**

A **context reader** is a person whose phonetic and structural analysis skills are inadequate, but who is still able to extract meaning from the context of the material despite the inadequate decoding skills.

In addition to this inventory of Deon's strengths and weaknesses, we also know that he is independent in reading at a Preprimer level. Any reading that Deon is expected to do with no help from teacher or parent(s) should be at this level.

Deon is instructional at a Primer/first-grade reading level. Use Primer level and early first-grade level material for purposes of instructing Deon in the decoding area.

Avoid having Deon do any reading at the second-grade level, as this is his level of frustration; at least if he has to decode for himself.

Another way of looking at this discrepancy between Deon's level of decoding ability and his level of understanding is, for example, to take the word *cartoons*. Deon can say *cartoons* and he knows what the word *cartoons* means. He just doesn't know when he sees the word *cartoons* in print, that it's a word he knows, because he can't get it from print back into oral language where the meaning resides.

If the teacher can successfully remediate Deon's problems with decoding, Deon will be able to read at a fourth-grade level because we know from the Listening Capacity test that he has good comprehension at that level.

Sample CRI Record—Anna

Anna is a third-grade student who is 8 years, 10 months old. Her IQ, as measured by the Wechsler Intelligence Scale for Children–III, is in the low average range. Her grade equivalency in reading is 1.5, as measured by a group reading achievement test.

The score on the group reading achievement test is an indication that Anna's reading is below average for her grade level. The indication of below average reading, however, does not explain *why* Anna's reading is below average.

In order to determine why Anna's reading is not at grade level, Anna's teacher, Liz Sage, administered Form A: Pretest of the CRI to Anna. Her Inventory Record and Summary Sheet follow on pages 31 to 33. You also can follow along with Dr. Wheelock assessing Anna on the website *www.classroomreadinginventory.com*.

Getting Started—Graded Word Lists:

Ms. Sage: Anna, I have some words on these lists, and I want you to say them out loud for me. If you come to a word you don't know, it's OK to say "I don't know." Just do the best you can.

Ms. Sage then places the Form A: Pretest Preprimer-Primer (PP-P) Graded Word Lists in front of Anna, and pointing to the first word *this* on the Preprimer list says, "OK, start here."

As Anna decodes the words on these lists, Ms. Sage records her responses in the Inventory Record for Teachers, Form A. This procedure is followed with successive Graded Word Lists until the student misses five or more words in any column, at which point this part of the testing is stopped. Ms. Sage then moves on to the Graded Paragraphs.

Form A: Pretest Inventory Record
Summary Sheet

Student's Name: _____Anna J._____ Grade: ___3___ Age: __8-10__

year, months

Date: _11/11/10_ School: _____Troost E.S._____ Administered by: ___Liz Sage___

Part 1 Word Lists			Part 2 Graded Paragraphs			
Grade Level	Percentage of Words Correct	Word Recognition Errors		SIG WR	COMP	LC
		Consonants				
PP	100%	_____ consonants	PP			
		_____ blends				
P	100%	_____ digraphs	P	IND	IND	
		_____ endings				
1	95%	_____ compounds	1	IND	INST	
		_____ contractions				
2	95%		2	IND	FR	
		Vowels				
3	100%	_____ long	3			
		_____ short				
4	80%	_____ long/short oo	4			
		_____ vowel + r				
5	65%	_____ diphthong	5			
		_____ vowel comb.				
6	%	_____ a + l or w	6			
			7			
7	%	**Syllable**				
		_____ visual patterns	8			
		_____ prefix				
8	%	_____ suffix				

Word Recognition Reinforcement and Vocabulary Development

Estimated Levels

	Grade
Independent	_P_
Instructional	_1_ (range)
Frustration	_2_
Listening Capacity	_N.D._

Comp Errors
- ✓ Factual (F)
- ✓ Inference (I)
- ✓ Vocabulary (V)
- ✓ "Word Caller" (A student who reads without associating meaning)
- _____ Poor Memory

Summary of Specific Needs:

Form A: Pretest   Part 1   Graded Word Lists

PP		P		1		2	
1. this	✓	1. came	✓	1. new	✓	1. birthday	✓
2. her	✓	2. day	✓	2. leg	✓	2. free	✓
3. about	✓	3. big	✓	3. feet	*foot*	3. isn't	✓
4. to	✓	4. house	✓	4. hear	✓	4. beautiful	✓
5. are	✓	5. after	✓	5. food	✓	5. job	✓
6. you	✓	6. how	✓	6. learn	✓	6. elephant	✓
7. he	✓	7. put	✓	7. hat	✓	7. cowboy	✓
8. all	✓	8. other	✓	8. ice	✓	8. branch	✓
9. like	✓	9. went	✓	9. letter	✓	9. asleep	✓
10. could	✓	10. just	✓	10. green	✓	10. mice	✓
11. my	✓	11. play	✓	11. outside	✓	11. corn	✓
12. said	✓	12. many	✓	12. happy	✓	12. baseball	✓
13. was	✓	13. trees	✓	13. less	✓	13. garden	✓
14. look	✓	14. boy	✓	14. drop	✓	14. hall	✓
15. go	✓	15. good	✓	15. stopping	✓	15. pet	✓
16. down	✓	16. girl	✓	16. grass	✓	16. blows	⬭(S)
17. with	✓	17. see	✓	17. street	✓	17. gray	✓
18. what	✓	18. something	✓	18. page	✓	18. law	✓
19. been	✓	19. little	✓	19. ever	✓	19. bat	✓
20. on	✓	20. saw	✓	20. let's	✓	20. guess	✓
	_100%_		_100%_		_95%_		_95%_

Teacher note: If the child misses five words in any column—stop Part 1. Begin Graded Paragraphs, Part 2 (Form A: Pretest) at the highest level in which the child recognized all 20 words. Each correct response equals 5%.

Form A: Pretest   Part 1   Graded Word Lists

3		4		5		6	
1. distant	✓	1. drain	✓	1. moan	_moon_	1. brisk	____
2. phone	✓	2. jug	✓	2. hymn	_hum_	2. nostrils	____
3. turkeys	✓	3. innocent	_P_	3. bravely	✓	3. dispose	____
4. bound	✓	4. relax	✓	4. instinct	_instric_	4. headlight	____
5. chief	✓	5. goodness	✓	5. shrill	✓	5. psychology	____
6. foolish	✓	6. seventeen	✓	6. jewel	✓	6. farthest	____
7. engage	✓	7. disturb	_dis-trub_	7. onion	✓	7. wreath	____
8. glow	✓	8. glove	✓	8. register	✓	8. emptiness	____
9. unhappy	✓	9. compass	✓	9. embarrass	_P_	9. billows	____
10. fully	✓	10. attractive	✓	10. graceful	✓	10. mob	____
11. court	✓	11. impact	✓	11. cube	_cub_	11. biblical	____
12. energy	✓	12. lettuce	✓	12. scar	✓	12. harpoon	____
13. passenger	✓	13. operator	✓	13. muffled	✓	13. pounce	____
14. shark	✓	14. regulation	✓	14. pacing	_passing_	14. rumor	____
15. vacation	✓	15. violet	✓	15. oars	✓	15. dazzle	____
16. pencil	✓	16. settlers	✓	16. guarantee	✓	16. combustion	____
17. labor	✓	17. polite	_police_	17. thermometer	✓	17. hearth	____
18. decided	✓	18. internal	_in-tern-nal_	18. zone	✓	18. mockingbird	____
19. policy	✓	19. drama	✓	19. salmon	_sal-mon_	19. ridiculous	____
20. nail	✓	20. landscape	✓	20. magical	✓	20. widen	____
	_100%_		_80%_		_65%_		____%

Teacher note: If the child misses five words in any column—stop Part 1. Begin Graded Paragraphs, Part 2 (Form A: Pretest) at the highest level in which the child recognized all 20 words. Each correct response equals 5%.

Scoring and Interpretation for Sample CRI—Anna

Part 1 Graded Words Lists—Scoring

- At the Preprimer (PP) level, Anna decoded all twenty words correctly. Score = 100%.

- At the Primer (P) level, Anna decoded all twenty words correctly. Score = 100%.

- At Level 1 (first grade), Anna said *foot* for *feet*. Score = 95%.

- At Level 2 (second grade), Anna omitted the *s* ending of the word *blows*. Score = 95%.

- At Level 3 (third grade), Anna decoded all twenty words correctly. Score = 100%.

- At Level 4 (fourth grade), Anna did not recognize word number 3 *innocent*. Therefore, Ms. Sage pronounced the word *innocent* for Anna to maintain the flow and marked *P* for pronounced. Anna decoded *disturb* with a nonsense word *dis-trub*, said *police* for *polite*, and said *in-tern-nal* for *internal*. Score = 80%.

- At Level 5 (fifth grade), Anna said *moon* for *moan*, and *hum* for *hymn*, and decoded *instinct* with a nonsense word *instric*. She failed to decode *embarrass*, and Ms. Sage pronounced it for her. Anna said *cub* for *cube*, *passing* for *pacing*, and *sal-mon* for *salmon*. Score = 65%.

- Part 1 is now completed because Anna scored at 65%.

Part 1 Graded Word Lists—Interpretation

- For a third grader, Anna's phonetic and structural analysis skills appear to be well established. Some of the words Anna miscued may be due to a lack of experience with a word with an irregular pronunciation; e.g., not knowing that the *l* in *salmon* is silent.

- Let us now proceed to Part 2 Graded Paragraphs. Ms. Sage will start Anna at the Primer (P) level as that's the level where Anna had all twenty words decoded correctly on Part 1 Graded Word Lists. Dr. Wheelock models this case study in Anna's video on the website *www.classroomreadinginventory.com*.

Getting Started—Graded Paragraphs:

Ms. Sage: Anna, on this next part I have some stories that I want you to read out loud to me. After you finish a story, I will ask you some questions about what you read.

At this point, Ms. Sage introduces the primer story "Our Bus Ride" and completes the Background Knowledge Assessment by saying, "Has your class ever taken a field trip? Tell me about a field trip."

Once the Background Knowledge Assessment has been completed, Ms. Sage says, "Fine, Anna. Now, read this story out loud to me. It is called "Our Bus Ride."

When Anna finishes reading "Our Bus Ride," Ms. Sage removes the story from view and asks Anna the five questions.

This procedure is followed with successive stories until the student reaches the frustration level in word recognition and/or comprehension.

Background Knowledge Assessment: Has your class ever taken a field trip? Tell me about a field trip.

Adequate [✓]   Inadequate [   ]

OUR BUS RIDE

The children were all talking.

"No more talking, children," said Mrs. Brown.

"It is time for our trip."

"It is time to go to the farm."

Mrs. Brown said, "Get ~~in~~ on the bus."

"Please do not push anyone."

"We are ready to go now."

The children climbed into the bus.

Away went the bus.

It was a good day for a trip.

Comprehension Check

(F) 1. __✓__   Where are they going?
(Farm)

(F) 2. __✓__   How are they going?
(By bus)

(I) 3. __✓__   Who do you think
Mrs. Brown is?
(Teacher, bus driver, a parent)

(F) 4. __✓__   How did the children know
that it was time for the bus to
leave?
(Mrs. Brown said, "We are
ready to go now.")

(I) 5. _D.K._   Why do you think
Mrs. Brown asked the children
not to push anyone?
(Prevent accidents, any other
reasonable answer)

Scoring Guide   Primer

SIG WR Errors		COMP Errors	
(IND)	0	(IND)	0–1
INST	3	INST	$1\frac{1}{2}$–2
FRUST	6+	FRUST	$2\frac{1}{2}$ +

Form A: Pretest   Part 2/Level 1 (71 Words)

Background Knowledge Assessment: This story is about puppies. What can you tell me about puppies?

Adequate [✓]   Inadequate [ ]

MARIA'S PUPPIES

Maria has two puppies.

She thinks that puppies are fun to watch.

The puppies' names are *Sissy* and *Sassy*.

Puppies are born with their eyes closed.

Their ears are closed, too.

This is why they use their smell and touch.

After two weeks, puppies begin to open their eyes and ears.

Most puppies can bark after four weeks.

Maria knows that *Sissy* and *Sassy* will grow up
and
~~to~~ be good pets.

.

Comprehension Check

(F) 1. ___✓___ How many puppies does Maria have?
(Two)

(F) 2. ___1/2___ What are the puppies' names?
(Sissy and <u>Sassy</u>)

(I) 3. ___✓___ Why do you think that Maria thinks puppies are fun to watch?
(Any reasonable answer; e.g., they jump, roll around, chase their tails)

(F) 4. ___✓___ What can puppies do after four weeks?
(Bark)

(F) 5. ___D.K.___ At birth, puppies must use their sense of smell and touch. Why?
(Eyes or ears closed)

Scoring Guide   First

SIG WR Errors		COMP Errors	
(IND)	0	IND	0–1
INST	3	(INST)	1½–2
FRUST	6+	FRUST	2½+

Form A: Pretest   Part 2/Level 2 (76 Words)

Background Knowledge Assessment: What kinds of shows do you like to watch on TV?

Adequate [✓]   Inadequate [ ]

HOMEWORK FIRST

Marco and his sister Teresa love to watch TV.

The shows they like best are cartoons.

Every day after school they go outside ~~to~~ *and* play.

Soon, Mother calls to them to come in.

"It's time to do your homework," she says.

"When you finish your homework you can

watch your cartoons," Mother promises.

"Remember! Homework first."

Marco and Teresa are happy with this.

They do their homework.

Now they are ready to watch their ~~cartoon~~

shows.

Comprehension Check

(F) 1. ___—___ What do Marco and Teresa do first when they come home? (They go outside and play) *homework*

(F) 2. ___✓___ What did their mother promise them? (When they finish their homework they can watch cartoons [TV])

(V) 3. ___D.K.___ What does *promise* mean? (To do what you say you will do; or any other reasonable answer)

(F) 4. ___✓___ What kinds of shows do Marco and Teresa like to watch the most? (Cartoons)

(I) 5. ___—___ Other than cartoons, what shows do you think Marco and Teresa watch? *Scooby Doo* (Any reasonable answer; e.g., movies, MTV, sports)

Scoring Guide   Second

SIG WR Errors		COMP Errors	
(IND)	2	IND	0–1
INST	4	INST	$1\frac{1}{2}$–2
FRUST	8+	(FRUST)	$2\frac{1}{2}$ +

Scoring and Interpretation for Sample CRI—Anna

Part 2 Graded Paragraphs—Scoring

Anna read aloud the Primer story. Because her only word recognition error (Anna said *on* for *in*) is a low-weighted (insignificant) error, Anna is considered to be independent for word recognition. Anna answered all but one of the questions correctly, so she is judged to be independent in comprehension.

In reading the First Grade story, Anna made one insignificant word recognition error; she said *and* for *to*. She is considered to be independent for word recognition. Anna was able to recall only one of the puppies' names, so she received one-half credit. In addition, she was unable to answer question number 5, so she is judged to be instructional in comprehension.

Anna read the Second Grade story and made two low-weighted miscues; she said *and* for *to*, and omitted the word *their*. Anna is considered to be independent in word recognition. Anna missed three of the five questions, so she is judged to be at the frustration level in comprehension.

From the number of missed questions Anna made with the first- and second-grade stories, it is clear that she has reached frustration level with comprehension. No further testing is done.

Because Anna has reached the frustration level due to a problem with comprehension, the Listening Capacity Format is *not* used. The Listening Capacity Format is used only when a student's below average achievement in reading is due to a word recognition problem, and not a problem with comprehension.

Part 2 Graded Paragraphs—Interpretation

The results of Anna's testing on the CRI indicate a problem with comprehension. Anna appears to have difficulty with all areas of comprehension—factual/literal, vocabulary, and inferential/critical reading. Her phonetic and structural analysis skills, however, are well established for a third grader. Anna is a **word caller.** A **word caller** is a student whose decoding skills are well established but who does not assign meaning to what is decoded.

In addition to this inventory of Anna's strengths and weaknesses, we also know that she is independent in reading at a Primer reading level. Any reading that Anna is expected to do with no help from teacher or parent(s) should be at this level.

Anna is instructional at a first-grade reading level. Use first grade level material for purposes of instructing Anna in the comprehension area.

Avoid having Anna do any reading at the second-grade level, as this is her level of frustration; at least if she has to associate meaning with what she reads.

SUBSKILLS FORMAT
FORM A: PRETEST

PART 1 Graded Word Lists

Form A: Pretest   Graded Word Lists

1.	this		1.	came
2.	her		2.	day
3.	about		3.	big
4.	in		4.	house
5.	are		5.	after
6.	you		6.	saw
7.	see		7.	put
8.	all		8.	under
9.	like		9.	went
10.	blue		10.	must
11.	my		11.	please
12.	said		12.	many
13.	was		13.	trees
14.	look		14.	boy
15.	go		15.	good
16.	come		16.	girl
17.	with		17.	ran
18.	away		18.	something
19.	bank		19.	little
20.	on		20.	saw

Form A: Pretest   Graded Word Lists

1.	fly	1.	birthday
2.	leg	2.	sing
3.	feet	3.	it's
4.	hear	4.	beautiful
5.	food	5.	job
6.	think	6.	elephant
7.	hat	7.	cowboy
8.	ice	8.	branch
9.	letter	9.	asleep
10.	green	10.	mice
11.	outside	11.	corn
12.	happy	12.	baseball
13.	less	13.	garden
14.	stop	14.	hall
15.	giving	15.	best
16.	grass	16.	blows
17.	street	17.	cold
18.	page	18.	law
19.	walk	19.	bat
20.	let's	20.	found

Form A: Pretest   Graded Word Lists

1.	distant		1.	drain
2.	phone		2.	jug
3.	turkeys		3.	innocent
4.	about		4.	relax
5.	clean		5.	goodness
6.	foolish		6.	seventeen
7.	engage		7.	disrespect
8.	show		8.	frown
9.	unhappy		9.	compass
10.	better		10.	attractive
11.	court		11.	fabric
12.	energy		12.	lettuce
13.	passenger		13.	operator
14.	start		14.	multiplication
15.	vacation		15.	violet
16.	pencil		16.	settlers
17.	labor		17.	polite
18.	decided		18.	internal
19.	policy		19.	drama
20.	nail		20.	toothbrush

Form A: Pretest   Graded Word Lists

1.	moan	1.	brisk
2.	hymn	2.	nostrils
3.	bravely	3.	compromise
4.	voyage	4.	headlight
5.	shrill	5.	hypothesis
6.	jewel	6.	farthest
7.	chocolate	7.	wreath
8.	register	8.	emptiness
9.	classify	9.	billows
10.	graceful	10.	mob
11.	cube	11.	calculate
12.	scar	12.	harpoon
13.	muffled	13.	pounce
14.	pacing	14.	rumor
15.	toe	15.	dazzle
16.	guarantee	16.	relationship
17.	thermometer	17.	hearth
18.	erode	18.	international
19.	salmon	19.	ridiculous
20.	magical	20.	widen

Form A: Pretest   Graded Word Lists

1.	proven		1.	utilization
2.	founder		2.	valve
3.	motivate		3.	rehabilitate
4.	glorify		4.	kidnapper
5.	adoption		5.	offensive
6.	darted		6.	ghetto
7.	nimble		7.	bewildered
8.	sanitation		8.	discourse
9.	enthusiastic		9.	vanity
10.	unravel		10.	radiant
11.	pompous		11.	horrid
12.	knapsack		12.	vastly
13.	bankruptcy		13.	strenuous
14.	geological		14.	greedy
15.	stockade		15.	sanctuary
16.	kerchief		16.	quartet
17.	snarl		17.	miser
18.	obtainable		18.	indignant
19.	hysterical		19.	scallop
20.	basin		20.	gradient

SUBSKILLS FORMAT
FORM A: PRETEST

PART 2 Graded Paragraphs

THE PLAY CAR

Tom has a play car.

His play car is red.

"See my play car," said Tom.

"It can go fast."

Ann said, "It's a big car."

"I like your car."

"Good," said Tom.

"Would you like a ride?"

OUR BUS RIDE

The children were all talking.

"No more talking, children," said Mrs. Brown.

"It is time for our trip."

"It is time to go to the farm."

Mrs. Brown said, "Get in the bus."

"Please do not push anyone."

"We are ready to go now."

The children climbed into the bus.

Away went the bus.

It was a good day for a trip.

MARIA'S PUPPIES

Maria has two puppies.

She thinks that puppies are fun to watch.

The puppies' names are *Sissy* and *Sassy.*

Puppies are born with their eyes closed.

Their ears are closed, too.

This is why they use their smell and touch.

After two weeks, puppies begin to open their eyes and ears.

Most puppies can bark after four weeks.

Maria knows that *Sissy* and *Sassy* will grow up to be good pets.

HOMEWORK FIRST

Marco and his sister Teresa love to watch TV.

The shows they like best are cartoons.

Every day after school they go outside to play.

Soon, Mother calls to them to come in.

"It's time to do your homework," she says.

"When you finish your homework you can watch your cartoons," Mother promises.

"Remember! Homework first."

Marco and Teresa are happy with this.

They do their homework.

Now they are ready to watch their cartoon shows.

LOOK AT THE SKY!

"Look at that sky!" shouted Sammie as he pointed upward. Suddenly a funnel like a monster's tail dropped out of the heavy clouds. Sammie grabbed Max's hand and yelled, "Run to the bridge! It's a tornado!"

Now The wind sounded like cattle chasing them. Sammie remembered the fear he'd felt when a farm steer had charged him. A cowboy had pulled him to safety. Now he was the brave cowboy.

Max saw the funnel on the ground. Leaves, branches and grass tumbled in the air around them. There it was! The bridge was within sight! Sammie and Max threw themselves under it. Sammie covered Max's body and held onto rocks. The wind screamed and pounded them, and then it was still.

Were they alive? He knew they had escaped when Max threw his arms around his neck. Max hugged Sammie with all his might.

THE GOAT HERDER

Mr. Hezbah drove his dairy goats over the dry African path. Seth awakened with the coming of the bleating goats in the morning. The little bells around their necks chimed. Seth longed to go with Mr. Hezbah. Mr. Hezbah was old and bent, and Seth wanted to help him.

Perhaps Mr. Hezbah would pay him with a young female goat in the spring. Perhaps he could raise the goat to produce milk. Perhaps he would sell the goat milk to buy clothes and supplies to attend school. Yes, he decided with a laugh, one little goat could change his life.

Seth saw Mr. Hezbah and the goats turn the bend. He said in his strongest voice, "Good morning, Mr. Hezbah! I am very good with animals. May I help you herd the goats? Mr. Hezbah stopped and smiled. Would this be the day that changed Seth's life?

IF GIVEN THE OPPORTUNITY

Mae Carol Jemison was born in 1956. Her parents, a carpenter and a teacher, had high hopes for her. But she was to achieve more than they ever imagined.

Young Mae Jemison had a passion to be a pioneer beyond the earth's horizon. Mae also had interests including dance, acting, and civil rights, both in high school and college. She achieved degrees in chemical engineering and medicine. Later, she practiced medicine in Africa.

After these accomplishments, Dr. Mae Jemison decided to pursue her childhood dream. She was one of 15 people chosen to become astronauts from a field of over 2,000. Dr. Jemison became the first African American woman ever admitted into the U.S. astronaut program. She flew into space aboard the U.S. Space Shuttle *Endeavour* on September 12, 1992.

Following her historic flight and fame, Mae Jemison said that society should recognize how much all individuals can contribute if given the opportunity.

BORN A SLAVE

He was born a slave on a farm in Missouri. When he was still a baby, his father was killed in an accident. His mother was kidnapped by night raiders. As a child, he was raised by Moses and Susan Carver. They were his owners. They named him George Washington Carver.

Mr. and Mrs. Carver taught George to read and write as a boy. He was very eager to learn, and showed a great interest in plants. When he was eleven years old he went to a school for black children in Neosho, Missouri.

For the next 20 years, Carver worked hard to pay for his education. George became a scientist and won worldwide fame for his agricultural research. He was widely praised for his work with peanuts. He found over 300 uses for peanuts. He also spent a great deal of time helping to improve race relations.

Carver got many awards for his work. The George Washington Carver National Monument was established on 210 acres of the Missouri farm where he was born.

THE OLD ONES

There is only one place in the United States where four states meet. It is the vast Four Corners region where Arizona, Colorado, New Mexico, and Utah come together.

The Four Corners region is a beautiful landscape of canyons, of flat mesas rising above broad valleys. It is slickrock desert and red dust and towering cliffs and the lonely sky.

About 2,000 years ago, a group of men and women the Navajo people call the *Anasazi* moved into this area. *Anasazi* is a Navajo word; it means "the Old Ones."

At first, the Anasazi dug out pits, and they lived in these "pit" houses. Later, they began to build houses out of stone and adobe called *pueblos*. They built their pueblos in and on the cliffs.

The Anasazi lived in these cliff houses for centuries. They farmed corn, raised children, created pottery, and traded with other pueblos.

These once great pueblos have been empty since the last years of the thirteenth century, for the Anasazi walked away from homes that had been theirs for 700 years.

Who were the Anasazi? Where did they come from? Where did they go? They simply left, and the entire Four Corners region lay silent, seemingly empty for 500 years.

ALIENS IN THE EVERGLADES

Not long ago, a group of very surprised tourists suddenly came face-to-face with an alligator wildly fighting a large Burmese python in the Florida Everglades. Ten feet long, the native alligator battled against the bigger snake. Fully grown, these snakes can weigh 300 pounds and are over 17 feet long.

Burmese python first appeared in the Everglades in 1995. Many think that they were freed in this park by their owners. Others believe that they escaped pet stores and homes during Hurricane Andrew in 1992.

Alien species like the python do not have natural enemies in their new homes. They are a danger because they disrupt the food chain. Ultimately, it may be impossible to get rid of environmental troublemakers like the python once they have established themselves in a new habitat.

Many other incompatible species have escaped to the wild of the Everglades, including parakeets, swamp eels and squirrel monkeys. Consequently, Florida now also has more exotic lizard species than there are native lizards in the entire Southwest United States.

SUBSKILLS FORMAT
FORM A: PRETEST

Inventory Record for Teachers

Permission is granted by the publisher to reproduce pp. 61 through 74.

Form A: Pretest Inventory Record
Summary Sheet

Student's Name: _____ **Grade:** _____ **Age:** _____
year, months

Date: _____ **School:** _____ **Administered by:** _____

Part 1 Word Lists			Part 2 Graded Paragraphs			
Grade Level	**Percentage of Words Correct**	**Word Recognition Errors**		**SIG WR**	**COMP**	**LC**
PP	____ %	**Consonants** ____ consonants ____ blends	PP			
P	____ %	____ digraphs ____ endings	P			
1	____ %	____ compounds ____ contractions	1			
2	____ %		2			
3	____ %	**Vowels** ____ long	3			
4	____ %	____ short ____ long/short oo	4			
5	____ %	____ vowel + r ____ diphthong	5			
6	____ %	____ vowel comb. ____ a + l or w	6			
7	____ %	**Syllable**	7			
8	____ %	____ visual patterns ____ prefix ____ suffix	8			

Part 1 Word Lists (continued):

Word Recognition Reinforcement and Vocabulary Development

Estimated Levels   Grade

Independent   ____ /
Instructional   ____ / (range)
Frustration   ____ /
Listening Capacity   ____ /

Comp Errors
____ Factual (F)
____ Inference (I)
____ Vocabulary (V)
____ "Word Caller"
(A student who reads without associating meaning)
____ Poor Memory

Summary of Specific Needs:

Form A: Pretest   Part 1   Graded Word Lists

PP		P		1		2	
1. this	____	1. came	____	1. fly	____	1. birthday	____
2. her	____	2. day	____	2. leg	____	2. sing	____
3. about	____	3. big	____	3. feet	____	3. it's	____
4. in	____	4. house	____	4. hear	____	4. beautiful	____
5. are	____	5. after	____	5. food	____	5. job	____
6. you	____	6. saw	____	6. think	____	6. elephant	____
7. see	____	7. put	____	7. hat	____	7. cowboy	____
8. all	____	8. under	____	8. ice	____	8. branch	____
9. like	____	9. went	____	9. letter	____	9. asleep	____
10. blue	____	10. must	____	10. green	____	10. mice	____
11. my	____	11. please	____	11. outside	____	11. corn	____
12. said	____	12. many	____	12. happy	____	12. baseball	____
13. was	____	13. trees	____	13. less	____	13. garden	____
14. look	____	14. boy	____	14. stop	____	14. hall	____
15. go	____	15. good	____	15. giving	____	15. best	____
16. come	____	16. girl	____	16. grass	____	16. blows	____
17. with	____	17. ran	____	17. street	____	17. cold	____
18. away	____	18. something	____	18. page	____	18. law	____
19. bank	____	19. little	____	19. walk	____	19. bat	____
20. on	____	20. saw	____	20. let's	____	20. found	____
	____ %		____ %		____ %		____ %

Teacher note: If the child misses five words in any column—stop Part 1. Begin Graded Paragraphs, Part 2 (FORM A: Pretest), at the highest level in which the child recognized all 20 words. Each correct response equals 5%.

Form A: Pretest   Part 1   Graded Word Lists

3		4		5		6	
1. distant	____	1. drain	____	1. moan	____	1. brisk	____
2. phone	____	2. jug	____	2. hymn	____	2. nostrils	____
3. turkeys	____	3. innocent	____	3. bravely	____	3. compromise	____
4. about	____	4. relax	____	4. voyage	____	4. headlight	____
5. clean	____	5. goodness	____	5. shrill	____	5. hypothesis	____
6. foolish	____	6. seventeen	____	6. jewel	____	6. farthest	____
7. engage	____	7. disrespect	____	7. chocolate	____	7. wreath	____
8. show	____	8. frown	____	8. register	____	8. emptiness	____
9. unhappy	____	9. compass	____	9. classify	____	9. billows	____
10. better	____	10. attractive	____	10. graceful	____	10. mob	____
11. court	____	11. fabric	____	11. cube	____	11. calculate	____
12. energy	____	12. lettuce	____	12. scar	____	12. harpoon	____
13. passenger	____	13. operator	____	13. muffled	____	13. pounce	____
14. start	____	14. multiplication	____	14. pacing	____	14. rumor	____
15. vacation	____	15. violet	____	15. toe	____	15. dazzle	____
16. pencil	____	16. settlers	____	16. guarantee	____	16. relationship	____
17. labor	____	17. polite	____	17. thermometer	____	17. hearth	____
18. decided	____	18. internal	____	18. erode	____	18. international	____
19 policy	____	19 drama	____	19 salmon	____	19 ridiculous	____
20. nail	____	20. toothbrush	____	20. magical	____	20. widen	____
	____ %		____ %		____ %		____ %

Teacher note: If the child misses five words in any column—stop Part 1. Begin Graded Paragraphs, Part 2 (FORM A: Pretest), at the highest level in which the child recognized all 20 words. Each correct response equals 5%.

Form A: Pretest   Graded Word Lists

7

1. proven ____
2. founder ____
3. motivate ____
4. glorify ____
5. adoption ____
6. darted ____
7. nimble ____
8. sanitation ____
9. enthusiastic ____
10. unravel ____
11. pompous ____
12. knapsack ____
13. bankruptcy ____
14. geological ____
15. stockade ____
16. kerchief ____
17. snarl ____
18. obtainable ____
19. hysterical ____
20. basin ____

____%

8

1. utilization ____
2. valve ____
3. rehabilitate ____
4. kidnapper ____
5. offensive ____
6. ghetto ____
7. bewildered ____
8. discourse ____
9. vanity ____
10. radiant ____
11. horrid ____
12. vastly ____
13. strenuous ____
14. greedy ____
15. sanctuary ____
16. quartet ____
17. miser ____
18. indignant ____
19. scallop ____
20. gradient ____

____%

Teacher note: If the child misses five words in any column—stop Part 1. Begin Graded Paragraphs, Part 2 (FORM A: Pretest), at the highest level in which the child recognized all 20 words. Each correct response equals 5%.

Form A: Pretest   Part 2/Level PP (38 Words)

Background Knowledge Assessment: This story is about two children and a play car. Tell me what you think the children are doing.

Adequate ☐   Inadequate ☐

THE PLAY CAR

Tom has a play car.

His play car is red.

"See my play car," said Tom.

"It can go fast."

Ann said, "It's a big car."

"I like your car."

"Good," said Tom.

"Would you like a ride?"

Comprehension Check

(F) 1. _____ What are the names of the boy and girl in this story?
(Tom and Ann)

(F) 2. _____ What were they talking about?
(The play car)

(F) 3. _____ Who owns the play car?
(Tom)

(F) 4. _____ What color is the car?
(Red)

(I) 5. _____ What do you think Tom likes about the car?
(It is big, fast)

Scoring Guide   Preprimer

SIG WR Errors		COMP Errors	
IND	0	IND	0–1
INST	2	INST	$1\frac{1}{2}$–2
FRUST	4+	FRUST	$2\frac{1}{2}$+

Form A: Pretest   Part 2/Level P (62 Words)

Background Knowledge Assessment: Has your class ever taken a field trip? Tell me about a field trip.

Adequate [   ]   Inadequate [   ]

OUR BUS RIDE

The children were all talking.

"No more talking, children," said Mrs. Brown.

"It is time for our trip."

"It is time to go to the farm."

Mrs. Brown said, "Get in the bus."

"Please do not push anyone."

"We are ready to go now."

The children climbed into the bus.

Away went the bus.

It was a good day for a trip.

Comprehension Check

(F) 1. _____ Where are they going?
(Farm)

(F) 2. _____ How are they going?
(By bus)

(I) 3. _____ Who do you think Mrs. Brown is?
(Teacher, bus driver, a parent)

(F) 4. _____ How did the children know that it was time for the bus to leave?
(Mrs. Brown said, "We are ready to go now.")

(I) 5. _____ Why do you think Mrs. Brown asked the children not to push anyone?
(Prevent accidents, any other reasonable answer)

Scoring Guide   Primer

SIG WR Errors		COMP Errors	
IND	0	IND	0–1
INST	3	INST	$1\frac{1}{2}$–2
FRUST	6+	FRUST	$2\frac{1}{2}$+

Form A: Pretest   Part 2/Level 1 (71 Words)

Background Knowledge Assessment: This story is about puppies. What can you tell me about puppies?

Adequate [ ]   Inadequate [ ]

MARIA'S PUPPIES

Maria has two puppies.

She thinks that puppies are fun to watch.

The puppies' names are *Sissy* and *Sassy*.

Puppies are born with their eyes closed.

Their ears are closed, too.

This is why they use their smell and touch.

After two weeks, puppies begin to open their

eyes and ears.

Most puppies can bark after four weeks.

Maria knows that *Sissy* and *Sassy* will grow up

to be good pets.

Comprehension Check

(F) 1. _____ How many puppies does Maria have?
(Two)

(F) 2. _____ What are the puppies' names?
(Sissy and Sassy)

(I) 3. _____ Why do you think that Maria thinks puppies are fun to watch?
(Any reasonable answer; e.g., they jump, roll around, chase their tails)

(F) 4. _____ What can puppies do after four weeks?
(Bark)

(F) 5. _____ At birth, puppies must use their sense of smell and touch. Why?
(Eyes or ears closed)

Scoring Guide   First

SIG WR Errors		COMP Errors	
IND	0	IND	0–1
INST	3	INST	$1\frac{1}{2}$–2
FRUST	6+	FRUST	$2\frac{1}{2}$+

Form A: Pretest   Part 2/Level 2 (76 Words)

Background Knowledge Assessment: What kinds of shows do you like to watch on TV?

Adequate ☐   Inadequate ☐

HOMEWORK FIRST

Marco and his sister Teresa love to watch TV.

The shows they like best are cartoons.

Every day after school they go outside to play.

Soon, Mother calls to them to come in.

"It's time to do your homework," she says.

"When you finish your homework you can

watch your cartoons," Mother promises.

"Remember! Homework first."

Marco and Teresa are happy with this.

They do their homework.

Now they are ready to watch their cartoon

shows.

Comprehension Check

(F) 1. _____ What do Marco and Teresa do first when they come home? (They go outside and play)

(F) 2. _____ What did their mother promise them? (When they finish their homework they can watch cartoons [TV])

(V) 3. _____ What does *promise* mean? (To do what you say you will do; or any other reasonable answer)

(F) 4. _____ What kinds of shows do Marco and Teresa like to watch the most? (Cartoons)

(I) 5. _____ Other than cartoons, what shows do you think Marco and Teresa watch? (Any reasonable answer; e.g., movies, MTV, sports)

Scoring Guide   Second

SIG WR Errors		COMP Errors	
IND	2	IND	0–1
INST	4	INST	$1^1/_2$–2
FRUST	8+	FRUST	$2^1/_2$+

Form A: Pretest   Part 2/Level 3 (125 Words)

Background Knowledge Assessment: Have you ever experienced a tornado or other big storm? Tell me how that experience made you feel.

Adequate [   ]   Inadequate [   ]

LOOK AT THE SKY!

"Look at that sky!" shouted Sammie as he pointed upward. Suddenly a funnel like a monster's tail dropped out of the heavy clouds. Sammie grabbed Max's hand and yelled, "Run to the bridge! It's a tornado!"

Now the wind sounded like cattle chasing them. Sammie remembered the fear he'd felt when a farm steer had charged him. A cowboy had pulled him to safety. Now he was the brave cowboy.

Max saw the funnel on the ground. Leaves, branches and grass tumbled in the air around them. There it was! The bridge was within sight! Sammie and Max threw themselves under it. Sammie covered Max's body and held onto rocks. The wind screamed and pounded them, and then it was still.

Were they alive? He knew they had escaped when Max threw his arms around his neck. Max hugged Sammie with all his might.

Comprehension Check

(F) 1. _____ What did Sammie see in the sky?
(A tornado; a funnel cloud like a monster's tail)

(F) 2. _____ What did the wind sound like?
(Cattle running; a steer chasing them; hoofs; stomping)

(V) 3. _____ What is a steer? (Cattle; cow)

(I) 4. _____ Why do you think Sammie and Max ran under the bridge?
(Any reasonable answer; e.g., the tornado would fly over; they would be protected)

(F) 5. _____ When did Sammy finally know that he and Max had escaped from the tornado?
(When Max threw his arms around his neck; when Max hugged him)

Scoring Guide   Third

SIG WR Errors		COMP Errors	
IND	2	IND	0–1
INST	7	INST	1½–2
FRUST	14	FRUST	2½ +

Form A: Pretest   Part 2/Level 4 (166 Words)

Background Knowledge Assessment: Tell me about something you'd like to do when you get older.

Adequate ☐   Inadequate ☐

THE GOAT HERDER

Mr. Hezbah drove his dairy goats over the dry African path. Seth awakened with the coming of the bleating goats in the morning. The little bells around their necks chimed. Seth longed to go with Mr. Hezbah. Mr. Hezbah was old and bent, and Seth wanted to help him.

Perhaps Mr. Hezbah would pay him with a young female goat in the spring. Perhaps he could raise the goat to produce milk. Perhaps he would sell the goat milk to buy clothes and supplies to attend school. Yes, he decided with a laugh, one little goat could change his life.

Seth saw Mr. Hezbah and the goats turn the bend. He said in his strongest voice, "Good morning, Mr. Hezbah! I am very good with animals. May I help you herd the goats? Mr. Hezbah stopped and smiled. Would this be the day that changed Seth's life?

Comprehension Check

(F) 1. _____ If Seth could get money for selling goat milk, what did he want to do with that money?
(Buy clothes and supplies to attend school)

(V) 2. _____ What does *herd* mean in the sentence, *May I help you herd the goats?*
(Any reasonable answer; e.g., keep the goats together as they walk; make sure the goats stay together as they eat; don't let any goats run away)

(F) 3. _____ On what continent did Mr. Hezbah and Seth live?
(Africa)

(I) 4. _____ Why did Seth think that going to school would change his life?
(Any reasonable answer related to education helping people have a better life)

(I) 5. _____ Why did Seth think Mr. Hezbah might need his help?
(Mr. Hezbah was old, bent; might have trouble keeping up with the goats or caring for goats)

Scoring Guide   Fourth

SIG WR Errors		COMP Errors	
IND	3	IND	0–1
INST	8	INST	1½–2
FRUST	16	FRUST	2½ +

Form A: Pretest   Part 2/Level 5 (158 Words)

Background Knowledge Assessment: Why do you think that some people are excited about becoming astronauts and traveling in space?

Adequate [ ]   Inadequate [ ]

IF GIVEN THE OPPORTUNITY

Mae Carol Jemison was born in 1956. Her parents, a carpenter and a teacher, had high hopes for her. But she was to achieve more than they ever imagined.

Young Mae Jemison had a passion to be a pioneer beyond the earth's horizon. Mae also had interests including dance, acting, and civil rights, both in high school and college. She achieved degrees in chemical engineering and medicine. Later, she practiced medicine in Africa.

After these accomplishments, Dr. Mae Jemison decided to pursue her childhood dream. She was one of 15 people chosen to become astronauts from a field of over 2,000. Dr. Jemison became the first African American woman ever admitted into the U.S. astronaut program. She flew into space aboard the U.S. Space Shuttle *Endeavour* on September 12, 1992.

Following her historic flight and fame, Mae Jemison said that society should recognize how much all individuals can contribute if given the opportunity.

Comprehension Check

(F) 1. _____ Dr. Jemison was the first African American woman ever admitted into what program?
(U.S. astronaut program; national astronaut program)

(F) 2. _____ How many days did Dr. Jemison spend in space on her first flight?
(Eight days)

(I) 3. _____ When Mae Jemison was a little girl, why do you think her parents may not have imagined that one day she would be an astronaut?
(Any reasonable answer; e.g. space travel hadn't happened at the time when she was born; no other African-American woman had been an astronaut)

(V) 4. _____ What does *passion* mean in this sentence: *But Mae Jemison had a passion for exploring space?*
(Any reasonable answer; e.g., excited about; very interested; enthusiastic)

(I) 5. _____ Why do you think that Mae may have been involved in civil rights activities in high school and college?
(Any reasonable answer related to opportunity; wanting a society in which all people have a chance to succeed)

Scoring Guide   Fifth

SIG WR Errors		COMP Errors	
IND	2	IND	0–1
INST	8	INST	1½–2
FRUST	17+	FRUST	2½ +

Form A: Pretest   Part 2/Level 6 (175 Words)

Background Knowledge Assessment: Had you heard about George Washington Carver before reading the story? What do you remember about him?

BORN A SLAVE

He was born a slave on a farm in Missouri. When he was still a baby, his father was killed in an accident. His mother was kidnapped by night raiders. As a child, he was raised by Moses and Susan Carver. They were his owners. They named him George Washington Carver.

Mr. and Mrs. Carver taught George to read and write as a boy. He was very eager to learn, and showed a great interest in plants. When he was eleven years old he went to a school for black children in Neosho, Missouri.

For the next 20 years, Carver worked hard to pay for his education. George became a scientist and won worldwide fame for his agricultural research. He was widely praised for his work with peanuts. He found over 300 uses for peanuts. He also spent a great deal of time helping to improve race relations.

Carver got many awards for his work. The George Washington Carver National Monument was established on 210 acres of the Missouri farm where he was born.

Adequate [   ]   Inadequate [   ]

Comprehension Check

(F) 1. _____ Where was George Washington Carver born? (Missouri)

(F) 2. _____ What did George become? (Scientist)

(I) 3. _____ Why do you think George became so interested in plants? (He grew up on a farm, or any other reasonable answer)

(V) 4. _____ What does the word *improve* mean? (To make something better)

(F) 5. _____ What was the plant that Carver worked most with? (The peanut)

Scoring Guide   Sixth

SIG WR Errors		COMP Errors	
IND	2	IND	0–1
INST	8	INST	$1\frac{1}{2}$–2
FRUST	17+	FRUST	$2\frac{1}{2}$+

Form A: Pretest   Part 2/Level 7 (207 Words)

Background Knowledge Assessment: This story is about some Native Americans called the Anasazi. The Anasazi once lived in the southwestern United States. What can you tell me about Native American Indians?

THE OLD ONES

Adequate [ ]   Inadequate [ ]

There is only one place in the United States where four states meet. It is the vast Four Corners region where Arizona, Colorado, New Mexico, and Utah come together.

The Four Corners region is a beautiful landscape of canyons, of flat mesas rising above broad valleys. It is slickrock desert and red dust and towering cliffs and the lonely sky.

About 2,000 years ago, a group of men and women the Navajo people call the *Anasazi* moved into this area. *Anasazi* is a Navajo word; it means "the Old Ones."

At first, the Anasazi dug out pits, and they lived in these "pit" houses. Later, they began to build houses out of stone and adobe called *pueblos*. They built their pueblos in and on the cliffs.

The Anasazi lived in these cliff houses for centuries. They farmed corn, raised children, created pottery, and traded with other pueblos.

These once great pueblos have been empty since the last years of the thirteenth century, for the Anasazi walked away from homes that had been theirs for 700 years.

Who were the Anasazi? Where did they come from? Where did they go? They simply left, and the entire Four Corners region lay silent, seemingly empty for 500 years.

Comprehension Check

(F) 1. _____ Name two of the states in the Four Corners region.
(Arizona, Colorado, New Mexico, or Utah)

(V) 2. _____ What is a *century*?
(100 years)

(I) 3. _____ Why do you think Navajo named these people "The Old Ones"?
(Because they were the people who lived there long before the Navajo did; or any other reasonable explanation)

(I) 4. _____ What do you think caused the Anasazi to leave their homes?
(Any reasonable explanation; e.g., bad weather, war, some natural disaster)

(F) 5. _____ How long ago was it when the Anasazi moved into the Four Corners region?
(About 2,000 years ago)

Scoring Guide   Seventh

SIG WR Errors		COMP Errors	
IND	2	IND	0–1
INST	11	INST	$1\frac{1}{2}$–2
FRUST	22+	FRUST	$2\frac{1}{2}$+

Form A: Pretest   Part 2/Level 8 (171 Words)

Background Knowledge Assessment: This story tells about animals that escape to habitats where they usually don't live. Tell me why you think this might be a problem.

Adequate ☐   Inadequate ☐

ALIENS IN THE EVERGLADES

Not long ago, a group of very surprised tourists suddenly came face-to-face with an alligator wildly fighting a large Burmese python in the Florida Everglades. Ten feet long, the native alligator battled against the bigger snake. Fully grown, these snakes can weigh 300 pounds and are over 17 feet long.

Burmese python first appeared in the Everglades in 1995. Many think that they were freed in this park by their owners. Others believe that they escaped pet stores and homes during Hurricane Andrew in 1992.

Alien species like the python do not have natural enemies in their new homes. They are a danger because they disrupt the food chain. Ultimately, it may be impossible to get rid of environmental troublemakers like the python once they have established themselves in a new habitat.

Many other incompatible species have escaped to the wild of the Everglades, including parakeets, swamp eels and squirrel monkeys. Consequently, Florida now also has more exotic lizard species than there are native lizards in the entire Southwest United States.

Comprehension Check

(V) 1. _____ What does *incompatible* mean in this story? (Any reasonable answer; e.g., not fitting in; unsuited for; conflicting with)

(F) 2. _____ The Everglades are in what state? (Florida)

(F) 3. _____ What do some people think is the reason that Burmese pythons are appearing in the Everglades? (They were freed in park by owners or escaped from pet stores and homes during Hurricane Andrew)

(I) 4. _____ What do you think might happen to the Everglades if the number of incompatible animals continue to grow? (Any reasonable answer, e.g., natural species would die off or be killed; food chain disrupted for all species to live; perhaps native species will adapt to protect themselves; new laws or regulations on pets)

(F) 5. _____ What is another incompatible species mentioned in this story that has escaped into the Everglades? (Parakeets, swamp eels, squirrel monkeys)

Scoring Guide   Eighth

SIG WR Errors		COMP Errors	
IND	2	IND	0–1
INST	8	INST	1½–2
FRUST	17+	FRUST	2½ +

SUBSKILLS FORMAT
FORM A: POSTTEST

PART 1 Graded Word Lists

Form A: Posttest   Graded Word Lists

1.	to		1.	three
2.	now		2.	find
3.	so		3.	because
4.	from		4.	who
5.	big		5.	their
6.	had		6.	before
7.	at		7.	more
8.	yellow		8.	turn
9.	of		9.	think
10.	three		10.	yes
11.	no		11.	these
12.	jump		12.	school
13.	but		13.	word
14.	has		14.	even
15.	if		15.	would
16.	as		16.	like
17.	have		17.	ride
18.	be		18.	white
19.	or		19.	never
20.	an		20.	your

1. maybe
2. pass
3. out
4. they
5. please
6. love
7. going
8. eight
9. kind
10. read
11. paid
12. over
13. top
14. pool
15. low
16. thank
17. every
18. short
19. just
20. us

1. sound
2. climb
3. waiting
4. hands
5. cry
6. doctor
7. people
8. everyone
9. write
10. inch
11. green
12. before
13. thirty
14. dance
15. test
16. hard
17. don't
18. story
19. city
20. wash

Form A: Posttest   Graded Word Lists

1.	computer		1.	spy
2.	laugh		2.	downtown
3.	energy		3.	tray
4.	choice		4.	skull
5.	hospital		5.	exhibit
6.	court		6.	formal
7.	heard		7.	weekend
8.	closet		8.	nineteen
9.	together		9.	mixture
10.	picnic		10.	invitation
11.	eight		11.	volunteer
12.	law		12.	gulf
13.	build		13.	rumble
14.	objects		14.	plot
15.	probably		15.	cotton
16.	shark		16.	weary
17.	we'll		17.	faucet
18.	paragraph		18.	conversation
19.	telephone		19.	weep
20.	today		20.	jelly

1.	solution		1.	vibrant
2.	exercise		2.	greatness
3.	funeral		3.	tardy
4.	practice		4.	doughnut
5.	mutual		5.	optimist
6.	surrounded		6.	nurture
7.	deliberately		7.	dismay
8.	officially		8.	shipment
9.	taxi		9.	logic
10.	parachute		10.	reinforce
11.	radar		11.	fingerprint
12.	intermediate		12.	jumbo
13.	embarrass		13.	ballot
14.	heart		14.	narrator
15.	crude		15.	crutch
16.	bakery		16.	shopper
17.	knelt		17.	punish
18.	endure		18.	silken
19.	painful		19.	omelet
20.	squash		20.	predicament

Form A: Posttest   Graded Word Lists

1.	noisily	1.	duly
2.	pyramid	2.	furnishing
3.	grieve	3.	emptiness
4.	foothills	4.	frustration
5.	nominate	5.	joyously
6.	include	6.	patriotic
7.	formulate	7.	devout
8.	enact	8.	seriousness
9.	depot	9.	affluent
10.	illegal	10.	federation
11.	distress	11.	youth
12.	childish	12.	selection
13.	unfair	13.	dismal
14.	eliminate	14.	somber
15.	athlete	15.	habitation
16.	luggage	16.	fling
17.	historically	17.	dungeon
18.	uncertainty	18.	hierarchy
19.	gardener	19.	replica
20.	enchant	20.	journalist

SUBSKILLS FORMAT
FORM A: POSTTEST

PART 2 Graded Paragraphs

FISHING

Bob and Pam went fishing.

Bob put his line in the water.

He felt something pull on his line.

"A fish! A fish!" said Bob.

"Help me get it, Pam."

Pam said, "It's a big one."

Bob said, "We can get it."

JOSÉ'S FIRST AIRPLANE RIDE

José and his papa went to the airport.

José was very happy.

His papa was happy, too.

They got on the airplane.

Up high into the sky they flew.

"How high we are," said José.

"The cars look so small."

"And so do the houses," said Papa.

José said, "This is so much fun."

PLANT SPIDERS

There are all kinds of spiders.

Some spiders are big, and some spiders are small.

One kind of spider is called a plant spider.

Plant spiders are black and green in color.

Plant spiders have eight legs.

All spiders have eight legs.

Plant spiders spin their webs on plants.

That is why they are called plant spiders.

They soon learn to hunt for food and spin their webs.

THE RODEO

It is a warm, sunny day. Many people have

come to the rodeo to see Bob Hill ride Midnight.

Bob Hill is one of the best cowboys in the rodeo.

Midnight is one of the best horses in the rodeo.

He is big and fast. Midnight is a strong black horse.

The people at the rodeo stand up.

They are all waiting for the big ride.

Can Bob Hill ride the great horse Midnight?

GREAT WALL OF CHINA

The Chinese began work on the Great Wall about 2,000 years ago. Over time, it became the largest wall ever built. The Great Wall is about 25 feet high with watchtowers used for lookout posts. The Great Wall is almost 4,000 miles long. It was built to keep China safe from invaders from the north.

For the most part, the Great Wall kept China safe from these enemies. However, the armies of the Mongol leader Genghis Khan did cross the wall 900 years ago and conquered most of China.

Today, the Chinese no longer use the wall for defense. Visitors from all over the world come to see the Great Wall and walk the path along its top.

The Great Wall of China is so big a structure that astronauts can see it as they orbit the earth.

MISS MILLY'S KITTY

Miss Milly was an elderly lady who lived in the oldest house in our neighborhood. This little house still had a barn in the back and a wood burning stove in the kitchen.

Miss Milly was quite a sight to see. She wore enormous purple hats and red paper flowers pinned to her apron. She sometimes looked like the scarecrow in her garden. Filled with energy, Miss Milly rode an odd bike made from pipes and old buggy wheels.

Wherever she went, Miss Milly brought along her pet chicken perched on her shoulder. Miss Milly called her chicken Kitty, and sometimes slipped us kids a warm, brown egg from her apron pocket.

This was long ago, but I still remember fondly my childhood friends, Miss Milly and a chicken named Kitty.

A CURIOUS MIND

Eleven-year-old Mario Molina leaned over his microscope. All kinds of creatures were moving under the lens that he could not see without the microscope. Soon he was working with a chemistry set and using his bathroom as a laboratory.

Years later, Mario was the first Mexican American to win a Nobel Prize in Chemistry. The Nobel Prize includes a large sum of money and a gold medal. It is one of the highest awards in the world. Mario was picked because of his discoveries about dangers of chemicals in the earth's ozone layer.

Young people have asked Dr. Molina what qualities they need to have to become scientists. "Most of all, you need to be curious and creative. You need to work hard and be patient. Most of all, enjoy what you do. If you are curious, creative, hard-working and patient, being a scientist will be fun and rewarding."

ALONG THE OREGON TRAIL

Today Missouri is in the central part of the United States. In 1800, it was not the center. In those days Missouri was on the edge of the frontier. Very few people had ever seen the great lands that lay to the west of Missouri.

In 1804, Captain Meriwether Lewis and William Clark set out from St. Louis to explore these lands. In November 1805, they reached the Pacific Ocean. The route they took later became known as the Oregon Trail.

When they returned, Lewis and Clark told many exciting stories about the West. This made other people want to make the West their home.

By the 1830s, settlers began making the long trip to the West. Missouri was the starting place for almost all these settlers. In the cities of Independence, St. Joseph, or Westport, they bought wagons, tools, and food for the two-thousand-mile trip. They went along the Oregon Trail through plains and deserts, over mountains, and across rivers.

TITANIC

The *Titanic* was the largest ship in the world. The *Titanic* was thought to be unsinkable.

On the night of April 14, 1912, the sea was calm, and the night was clear and cold. The *Titanic* was on its first trip from England to New York. The captain had received warnings of icebergs ahead. He decided to keep going at full speed and keep a sharp watch for any icebergs.

The men on watch aboard the *Titanic* saw an iceberg just ahead. It was too late to avoid it. The iceberg tore a 300-foot gash in the *Titanic*'s side. The ship sank in about 2½ hours.

Of the 2,200 passengers and crew, only 705 people were saved. They were mostly women and children.

In 1985, researchers from France and the United States found the *Titanic* at the bottom of the Atlantic Ocean. Sharks and other fish now swam along the decaying decks where joyful passengers once strolled.

THE DIARY

Anne Frank, a young Jewish girl, was born in Germany in 1929. A few years after Anne's birth, Adolf Hitler and the Nazi party came to power in Germany. Germany was in a great economic depression at the time, and Hitler blamed these problems on the Jews. To escape the persecution of the Nazis, Anne and her family, like many other Jews, fled to Holland. There in Amsterdam, Anne grew up in the 1930s and early 1940s.

For her thirteenth birthday, Anne received a diary. She began writing in it. In 1942, Hitler conquered Holland, and the Nazis soon began rounding up the Jews to send them to concentration camps. Millions of Jews died in these camps.

To escape the Nazis, the Franks went into hiding. Some of their Dutch friends hid Anne and her family in secret rooms above a warehouse in Amsterdam. In that small space the Franks lived secretly for more than two years. During that time, Anne continued to write in her diary.

By the summer of 1944, World War II was coming to an end. The American and British armies freed Holland from the Nazis, but not in time to save Anne and her family. Police discovered their hiding place and sent Anne and her family to concentration camps. Anne Frank died in the camp at Bergen-Belsen in March 1945. She was not yet sixteen years old.

All of the Franks died in the camps except Anne's father. After the war, Mr. Frank returned to Amsterdam. He revisited the small, secret rooms his family had hidden in for so long. Among the trash and broken furniture, he found Anne's diary.

SUBSKILLS FORMAT

FORM A: POSTTEST

Inventory Record for Teachers

Form A: Posttest Inventory Record
Summary Sheet

Student's Name: _____ Grade: _____ Age: _____

year, months

Date: _____ School: _____ Administered by: _____

Part 1 Word Lists			Part 2 Graded Paragraphs			

Part 1
Word Lists

Grade Level	Percentage of Words Correct	Word Recognition Errors
PP	_____ %	**Consonants**
		_____ consonants
P	_____ %	_____ blends
		_____ digraphs
1	_____ %	_____ endings
		_____ compounds
2	_____ %	_____ contractions
3	_____ %	**Vowels**
		_____ long
4	_____ %	_____ short
		_____ long/short oo
5	_____ %	_____ vowel + r
		_____ diphthong
6	_____ %	_____ vowel comb.
		_____ a + l or w
7	_____ %	**Syllable**
		_____ visual patterns
8	_____ %	_____ prefix
		_____ suffix
		Word Recognition Reinforcement and Vocabulary Development

Part 2
Graded Paragraphs

	SIG WR	COMP	LC
PP			
P			
1			
2			
3			
4			
5			
6			
7			
8			

Estimated Levels	Grade
Independent	_____ /
Instructional	_____ / (range)
Frustration	_____ /
Listening Capacity	_____ /

Comp Errors
_____ Factual (F)
_____ Inference (I)
_____ Vocabulary (V)
_____ "Word Caller"
(A student who reads without associating meaning)
_____ Poor Memory

Summary of Specific Needs:

Form A: Posttest   Part 1   Graded Word Lists

PP		P		1		2	
1. to	___	1. three	___	1. maybe	___	1. sound	___
2. now	___	2. find	___	2. pass	___	2. climb	___
3. so	___	3. because	___	3. out	___	3. waiting	___
4. from	___	4. who	___	4. they	___	4. hands	___
5. big	___	5. their	___	5. please	___	5. cry	___
6. had	___	6. before	___	6. love	___	6. doctor	___
7. at	___	7. more	___	7. going	___	7. people	___
8. yellow	___	8. turn	___	8. eight	___	8. everyone	___
9. of	___	9. think	___	9. kind	___	9. write	___
10. three	___	10. yes	___	10. read	___	10. inch	___
11. no	___	11. these	___	11. paid	___	11. green	___
12. jump	___	12. school	___	12. over	___	12. before	___
13. but	___	13. word	___	13. top	___	13. thirty	___
14. has	___	14. even	___	14. pool	___	14. dance	___
15. if	___	15. would	___	15. low	___	15. test	___
16. as	___	16. like	___	16. thank	___	16. hard	___
17. have	___	17. ride	___	17. every	___	17. don't	___
18. be	___	18. white	___	18. short	___	18. story	___
19. or	___	19. never	___	19. just	___	19. city	___
20. an	___	20. your	___	20. us	___	20. wash	___
___%		___%		___%		___%	

Teacher note: If the child misses five words in any column—stop Part 1. Begin Graded Paragraphs, Part 2 (FORM A: Posttest), at the highest level in which the child recognized all 20 words. Each correct response equals 5%.

Form A: Posttest   Part 1   Graded Word Lists

3	4	5	6
1. computer ___	1. spy ___	1. solution ___	1. vibrant ___
2. laugh ___	2. downtown ___	2. exercise ___	2. greatness ___
3. energy ___	3. tray ___	3. funeral ___	3. tardy ___
4. choice ___	4. skull ___	4. practice ___	4. doughnut ___
5. hospital ___	5. exhibit ___	5. mutual ___	5. optimist ___
6. court ___	6. formal ___	6. surrounded ___	6. nurture ___
7. heard ___	7. weekend ___	7. deliberately ___	7. dismay ___
8. closet ___	8. nineteen ___	8. officially ___	8. shipment ___
9. together ___	9. mixture ___	9. taxi ___	9. logic ___
10. picnic ___	10. invitation ___	10. parachute ___	10. reinforce ___
11. eight ___	11. volunteer ___	11. radar ___	11. fingerprint ___
12. law ___	12. gulf ___	12. intermediate ___	12. jumbo ___
13. build ___	13. rumble ___	13. embarrass ___	13. ballot ___
14. objects ___	14. plot ___	14. heart ___	14. narrator ___
15. probably ___	15. cotton ___	15. crude ___	15. crutch ___
16. shark ___	16. weary ___	16. bakery ___	16. shopper ___
17. we'll ___	17. faucet ___	17. knelt ___	17. punish ___
18. paragraph ___	18. conversation ___	18. endure ___	18. silken ___
19. telephone ___	19. weep ___	19. painful ___	19. omelet ___
20. today ___	20. jelly ___	20. squash ___	20. predicament ___
___ %	___ %	___ %	___ %

Teacher note: If the child misses five words in any column—stop Part 1. Begin Graded Paragraphs, Part 2 (FORM A: Posttest), at the highest level in which the child recognized all 20 words. Each correct response equals 5%.

Form A: Posttest

Graded Word Lists

7

1. noisily _____
2. pyramid _____
3. grieve _____
4. foothills _____
5. nominate _____
6. include _____
7. formulate _____
8. enact _____
9. depot _____
10. illegal _____
11. distress _____
12. childish _____
13. unfair _____
14. eliminate _____
15. athlete _____
16. luggage _____
17. historically _____
18. uncertainty _____
19. gardener _____
20. enchant _____

_____ %

8

1. duly _____
2. furnishing _____
3. emptiness _____
4. frustration _____
5. joyously _____
6. patriotic _____
7. devout _____
8. seriousness _____
9. affluent _____
10. federation _____
11. youth _____
12. selection _____
13. dismal _____
14. somber _____
15. habitation _____
16. fling _____
17. dungeon _____
18. hierarchy _____
19. replica _____
20. journalist _____

_____ %

Teacher note: If the child misses five words in any column—stop Part 1. Begin Graded Paragraphs, Part 2 (FORM A: Posttest), at the highest level in which the child recognized all 20 words. Each correct response equals 5%.

Form A: Posttest   Part 2/Level PP (43 Words)

Background Knowledge Assessment: This story is about two children who went fishing. Have you ever gone fishing? Tell me about it.

Adequate [   ]   Inadequate [   ]

FISHING

Bob and Pam went fishing.

Bob put his line in the water.

He felt something pull on his line.

"A fish! A fish!" said Bob.

"Help me get it, Pam."

Pam said, "It's a big one."

Bob said, "We can get it."

Comprehension Check

(F) 1. _____ What are the names of the boy and girl in this story?
(Bob and Pam)

(F) 2. _____ What were they doing?
(Fishing)

(F) 3. _____ What did Bob feel pull on his line?
(A fish)

(F) 4. _____ What did Pam say?
(It's a big one, a big fish)

(I) 5. _____ What do you think Bob and Pam did with the fish?
(Any reasonable answer; e.g., cooked it, let it go)

Scoring Guide   Preprimer

SIG WR Errors		COMP Errors	
IND	0	IND	0–1
INST	2	INST	$1\frac{1}{2}$–2
FRUST	4+	FRUST	$2\frac{1}{2}$+

Background Knowledge Assessment: Have you ever flown in an airplane? Tell me about it. If not, tell me what you think it might be like.

Adequate ☐   Inadequate ☐

JOSÉ'S FIRST AIRPLANE RIDE

José and his papa went to the airport.

José was very happy.

His papa was happy, too.

They got on the airplane.

Up high into the sky they flew.

"How high we are," said José.

"The cars look so small."

"And so do the houses," said Papa.

José said, "This is so much fun."

Comprehension Check

(F) 1. _____ Who is with José on the airplane? (Father, Papa)

(F) 2. _____ What words in the story told you that José liked his ride? (*José was very happy*; *This is so much fun*)

(V) 3. _____ What does the word *high* mean in this story? (Way up in the air, above the houses and cars)

(I) 4. _____ Why do you think José's papa took him for an airplane ride? (Any reasonable answer; e.g., because he had not been on an airplane before; they went to visit relatives)

(F) 5. _____ How many airplane rides did José have before this one? (None)

Scoring Guide   Primer

SIG WR Errors		COMP Errors	
IND	0	IND	0–1
INST	2	INST	$1\frac{1}{2}$–2
FRUST	5+	FRUST	$2\frac{1}{2}$+

Background Knowledge Assessment: This story is about spiders. What can you tell me about spiders?

Adequate [   ]   Inadequate [   ]

PLANT SPIDERS

There are all kinds of spiders.

Some spiders are big, and some spiders are

small.

One kind of spider is called a plant spider.

Plant spiders are black and green in color.

Plant spiders have eight legs.

All spiders have eight legs.

Plant spiders spin their webs on plants.

That is why they are called plant spiders.

They soon learn to hunt for food and spin

their webs.

Comprehension Check

(F) 1. _____   Are there more than one kind of
spider?
(Yes—many more)

(F) 2. _____   What color is the spider in this
story?
(Black and green)

(V) 3. _____   What does the word *plant*
mean in this story?
(Student gives an example of a
plant)

(I) 4. _____   What do you think spiders eat?
(Flies, bugs, insects)

(F) 5. _____   How many legs do all spiders
have?
(Eight)

Scoring Guide   First

SIG WR Errors		COMP Errors	
IND	0	IND	0–1
INST	3	INST	$1\frac{1}{2}$–2
FRUST	6+	FRUST	$2\frac{1}{2}$+

Background Knowledge Assessment: Have you ever been to a rodeo or seen one on TV? What do you know about rodeos?

Adequate [   ]   Inadequate [   ]

THE RODEO

It was a warm, sunny day. Many people have come to the rodeo to see Bob Hill ride Midnight. Bob Hill is one of the best cowboys in the rodeo. Midnight is one of the best horses in the rodeo. He is big and fast. Midnight is a strong black horse.

The people at the rodeo stood up. They are all waiting for the big ride. Can Bob Hill ride the great horse Midnight?

Comprehension Check

(F) 1. _____ What was the weather like on the day of the rodeo?
(Warm and sunny)

(I) 2. _____ The people seemed to be excited. Why?
(They wanted to see this great horse and/or cowboy)

(F) 3. _____ What was the name of the horse?
(Midnight)

(F) 4. _____ What did he (Midnight) look like?
(Big, fast, strong, black)

(I) 5. _____ Why do you think that Bob Hill was a good rider?
(Story said he was one of the best cowboys in the rodeo)

Scoring Guide   Second

SIG WR Errors		**COMP Errors**	
IND	0	IND	0–1
INST	3	INST	$1\frac{1}{2}$–2
FRUST	7+	FRUST	$2\frac{1}{2}$+

Background Knowledge Assessment: What do you know about China and/or the Great Wall of China?

Adequate ☐   Inadequate ☐

GREAT WALL OF CHINA

The Chinese began work on the Great Wall about 2,000 years ago. Over time, it became the largest wall ever built. The Great Wall is about 25 feet high with watchtowers used for lookout posts. The Great Wall is almost 4,000 miles long. It was built to keep China safe from invaders from the north.

For the most part, the Great Wall kept China safe from these enemies. However, the armies of the Mongol leader Genghis Khan did cross the wall 900 years ago and conquered most of China.

Today, the Chinese no longer use the wall for defense. Visitors from all over the world come to see the Great Wall and walk the path along its top.

The Great Wall of China is so big a structure that astronauts can see it as they orbit the earth.

Comprehension Check

(F) 1. _____   Why was the Great Wall of China built?
(To protect China from its enemies)

(F) 2. _____   How long is the Great Wall?
(About 4,000 miles long)

(I) 3. _____   Would you go to China to see the Great Wall? Why or why not?
(Any reasonable answer)

(V) 4. _____   What does the word *defense* mean?
(Protection, to protect someone or something)

(F) 5. _____   Who was Genghis Khan?
(The Mongol leader, the man who crossed the wall)

Scoring Guide   Third

SIG WR Errors		COMP Errors	
IND	1	IND	0–1
INST	7	INST	$1^1/_2$–2
FRUST	15+	FRUST	$2^1/_2$+

Background Knowledge Assessment: Have you ever met an interesting person you think you'll never forget? Tell me about it.

Adequate [ ]   Inadequate [ ]

MISS MILLY'S KITTY

Miss Milly was an elderly lady who lived in the oldest house in our neighborhood. This little house still had a barn in the back and a wood burning stove in the kitchen.

Miss Milly was quite a sight to see. She wore enormous purple hats and red paper flowers pinned to her apron. She sometimes looked like the scarecrow in her garden. Filled with energy, Miss Milly rode an odd bike made from pipes and old buggy wheels.

Wherever she went, Miss Milly brought along her pet chicken perched on her shoulder. Miss Milly called her chicken Kitty, and sometimes slipped us kids a warm, brown egg from her apron pocket.

This was long ago, but I still remember fondly my childhood friends, Miss Milly and a chicken named Kitty.

Comprehension Check

(F) 1. _____ What did Miss Milly ride as she traveled through the neighborhood?
(A bike)

(F) 2. _____ What did Miss Milly call her chicken?
(Kitty)

(V) 3. _____ What does *enormous* mean?
(Very big, very large, huge)

(I) 4. _____ Why do you think the person telling this story had such fond memories of Miss Milly and Kitty?
(Miss Milly and Kitty were fun to see; Miss Milly was so nice to neighborhood children; Miss Milly dressed and acted in an interesting way; any reasonable answer)

(F) 5. _____ What color were Miss Milly's hats?
(Purple)

Scoring Guide   Fourth

SIG WR Errors		COMP Errors	
IND	2	IND	0–1
INST	6	INST	1½–2
FRUST	12+	FRUST	2½ +

Form A: Posttest   Part 2/Level 5 (149 Words)

Background Knowledge Assessment: If you are curious about something you will want to learn more about it. Tell me about something that you are curious about.

Adequate [ ]   Inadequate [ ]

A CURIOUS MIND

Eleven-year-old Mario Molina leaned over his microscope. All kinds of creatures were moving under the lens that he could not see without the microscope. Soon he was working with a chemistry set and using his bathroom as a laboratory.

Years later, Mario was the first Mexican American to win a Nobel Prize in Chemistry. The Nobel Prize includes a large sum of money and a gold medal. It is one of the highest awards in the world. Mario was picked because of his discoveries about dangers of chemicals in the earth's ozone layer.

Young people have asked Dr. Molina what qualities they need to have to become scientists. "Most of all, you need to be curious and creative. You need to work hard and be patient. Most of all, enjoy what you do. If you are curious, creative, hard working and patient, being a scientist will be fun and rewarding."

Comprehension Check

(F) 1. _____ What room in his house did young Mario Molina use as a laboratory?
(His bathroom)

(F) 2. _____ What were one of the qualities that Dr. Molina thinks young people need if they want to become scientists?
(one of the following: Curious, creative, hard working, patient, enjoy what they do)

(V) 3. _____ What is a microscope?
(Something to see tiny creatures; science equipment that makes small things look larger; any reasonable explanation that identifies a microscope as something that magnifies objects)

(I) 4. _____ Why were Dr. Molina's discoveries about chemicals in the earth's ozone layer so important?
(Any reasonable explanation; e.g., chemicals can make us sick, hurt living things)

(I) 5. _____ Why do you think Mario's parents gave him a chemistry set and let him use the bathroom as a laboratory?
(Any reasonable answer, e.g., they saw his interest; love of science; wanted him to experiment to be a scientist)

Scoring Guide   Fifth

SIG WR Errors		COMP Errors	
IND	2	IND	0–1
INST	7	INST	1½–2
FRUST	15+	FRUST	2½ +

Background Knowledge Assessment: Two famous American explorers were Lewis and Clark. What do you know about them?

Adequate [   ]   Inadequate [   ]

ALONG THE OREGON TRAIL

Today Missouri is in the central part of the United States. In 1800, it was not the center. In those days Missouri was on the edge of the frontier. Very few people had ever seen the great lands that lay to the west of Missouri.

In 1804, Captain Meriwether Lewis and William Clark set out from St. Louis to explore these lands. In November 1805, they reached the Pacific Ocean. The route they took later became known as the Oregon Trail.

When they returned, Lewis and Clark told many exciting stories about the West. This made other people want to make the West their home.

By the 1830s, settlers began making the long trip to the West. Missouri was the starting place for almost all these settlers. In the cities of Independence, St. Joseph, or Westport, they bought wagons, tools, and food for the two-thousand-mile trip. They went along the Oregon Trail through plains and deserts, over mountains, and across rivers.

Comprehension Check

(F) 1. _____ From what city did Lewis and Clark set out to explore the West? (St. Louis)

(F) 2. _____ At the end of their long journey, what ocean did they reach? (Pacific Ocean)

(V) 3. _____ What is a *trail*? (Path, road, like a street)

(I) 4. _____ Why do you think people wanted to make the long trip West? (So they could have more land; they heard exciting stories about the West; or any other reasonable explanation)

(F) 5. _____ In what state are the cities of Independence and St. Joseph? (Missouri)

Scoring Guide   Sixth

SIG WR Errors		**COMP Errors**	
IND	2	IND	0–1
INST	8	INST	$1\frac{1}{2}$–2
FRUST	16+	FRUST	$2\frac{1}{2}$+

Form A: Posttest   Part 2/Level 7 (159 Words)

Background Knowledge Assessment: The *Titanic* is probably the most famous ship in the world. What can you tell me about the *Titanic*?

Adequate [   ]   Inadequate [   ]

TITANIC

The *Titanic* was the largest ship in the world. The *Titanic* was thought to be unsinkable.

On the night of April 14, 1912, the sea was calm, and the night was clear and cold. The *Titanic* was on its first trip from England to New York. The captain had received warnings of icebergs ahead. He decided to keep going at full speed and keep a sharp watch for any icebergs.

The men on watch aboard the *Titanic* saw an iceberg just ahead. It was too late to avoid it. The iceberg tore a 300-foot gash in the *Titanic*'s side. The ship sank in about $2\frac{1}{2}$ hours.

Of the 2,200 passengers and crew, only 705 people were saved. They were mostly women and children.

In 1985, researchers from France and the United States found the *Titanic* at the bottom of the Atlantic Ocean. Sharks and other fish now swam along the decaying decks where joyful passengers once strolled.

Comprehension Check

(V) 1. _____   What is an *iceberg*?
(It's like a mountain of ice; a huge pile of ice)

(F) 2. _____   What was the weather like on the night the *Titanic* sank?
(It was clear and cold)

(V) 3. _____   What does it mean to keep a *sharp watch*?
(To look for something very carefully; to be on the lookout for something)

(I) 4. _____   If you had the chance, would you want to go down and see the *Titanic*? Why or why not?
(Any reasonable explanation)

(F) 5. _____   Where was the *Titanic* going when it left England?
(New York)

Scoring Guide   Seventh

SIG WR Errors		COMP Errors	
IND	2	IND	0–1
INST	8	INST	$1\frac{1}{2}$–2
FRUST	15+	FRUST	$2\frac{1}{2}$+

Background Knowledge Assessment: Many people were killed by the Nazis during World War II. Perhaps one of the most famous was a young Jewish girl named Anne Frank. What do you know about Anne?

Adequate ☐   Inadequate ☐

THE DIARY

Anne Frank, a young Jewish girl, was born in Germany in 1929. A few years after Anne's birth, Adolf Hitler and the Nazi party came to power in Germany. Germany was in a great economic depression at the time, and Hitler blamed these problems on the Jews. To escape the persecution of the Nazis, Anne and her family, like many other Jews, fled to Holland. There in Amsterdam, Anne grew up in the 1930s and early 1940s.

For her thirteenth birthday, Anne received a diary. She began writing in it. In 1942, Hitler conquered Holland, and the Nazis soon began rounding up the Jews to send them to concentration camps. Millions of Jews died in these camps.

To escape the Nazis, the Franks went into hiding. Some of their Dutch friends hid Anne and her family in secret rooms above a warehouse in Amsterdam. In that small space the Franks lived secretly for more than two years. During that time, Anne continued to write in her diary.

By the summer of 1944, World War II was coming to an end. The American and British armies freed Holland from the Nazis, but not in time to save Anne and her family. Police discovered their hiding place and sent Anne and her family to concentration camps. Anne Frank died in the camp at Bergen-Belsen in March 1945. She was not yet sixteen years old.

All of the Franks died in the camps except Anne's father. After the war, Mr. Frank returned to Amsterdam. He revisited the small, secret rooms his family had hidden in for so long. Among the trash and broken furniture, he found Anne's diary.

Comprehension Check

(V) 1. _____ What does the word *persecution* mean? (To cause harm, suffering or death; to hunt down; to pursue)

(F) 2. _____ Who found Anne's diary? (Her father)

(F) 3. _____ Why did Anne and her family go into hiding? (To escape the Nazis)

(I) 4. _____ What do you think Anne wrote about in her diary? (Any reasonable answer; e.g., what it is like to be in hiding)

(I) 5. _____ How do you think the Nazis discovered the Franks' hiding place? (Someone told on them; the police searched all the buildings; or any other reasonable answer)

Scoring Guide   Eighth

SIG WR Errors		**COMP Errors**	
IND	3	IND	0–1
INST	11	INST	$1\frac{1}{2}$–2
FRUST	26+	FRUST	$2\frac{1}{2}$+

USING THE CRI:
SPECIFIC INSTRUCTIONS

For Administering the Reader Response Format
Form B: Pretest and Form B: Posttest

Introduction

The READER RESPONSE FORMAT is based on the following five assumptions.

1. The essential factors involved in *reading comprehension* are prior knowledge and prior experience.

2. The individual reader responses are affected by the reader's prior knowledge and experience.

3. The reader uses language (reader responses) to organize and reconstruct her prior knowledge and experience.

4. The reader is able to express prior knowledge and experience by making **Predictions** and **Retelling** the story, in his own words.

5. Finally, it is possible to assess the reader's ability to predict and retell and, thereby, gain valuable insights into the reader's ability to comprehend story material.

Thus, Form B: Reader Response Format is designed around the **Predicting** and **Retelling** of stories and divides these two essential factors into the following four scorable parts:

Student Ability	Scorable Parts
Predicting	1. *Predicting*—the use of the title to anticipate story or selection contents.
Retelling	2. *Character(s)*—the use of character(s) to deal with essential elements.
	3. *Problem(s)*—those elements used by the character(s) in the story to identify problem(s) or reach goal(s).
	4. *Outcome(s)*—usually deals with how the character(s) solved the problem(s) or attained the goal(s).

Prompting and Comfortable Reading Level

Prompting

To help assess a student's reading ability, teachers must become familiar with the concept of prompting. Teachers need to know how to prompt, when to prompt and how much to prompt.

EXAMPLE: Let's say you ask a student to define the word *hat*. The answer you are looking for is "A hat is something you wear on your head." The student's reply, however, is "A hat is something you wear." This is not a complete answer, so you prompt in a *general* way so as not to suggest the answer you want. You say to the student: "Tell me more about a hat." The student replies: "A hat is made of cloth." Still not the answer you are after. Now you prompt in a more *suggestive* way by saying: "Where do you wear a hat?" The student answers: "You wear a hat when you go outside." At this point the prompt becomes *specific,* and you say: "Yes, but on what part of your body do you wear a hat?" How much prompting does it take to arrive at the answer you deem necessary to indicate understanding on the student's part?

There are times when the teacher will guide the student by prompting. There are times when prompting is not necessary, and the teacher will not interrupt the free flow of reader response.

Reading Level

As the teacher listens to the student read and later discuss the story, is the student Independent (IND), Instructional (INST), or Frustration (FRUST) at a given grade level? What is meant by Independent, Instructional, and Frustration?

- *Independent:* The oral reading of the story is fluent and expressive; there are few, if any, significant word recognition errors. During the retelling, the student has no difficulty in recalling the character(s), or the problem(s) and the outcome(s)/solution(s). This is the student's independent level.

- *Instructional:* The oral reading of the selection is somewhat hesitant with an attempt at fluency; there are indications of an increasing number of significant word recognition errors. During the retelling, the student exhibits some difficulty in recalling the character(s), or the problem(s) and outcome(s)/solution(s). The teacher finds it necessary to do some *general* prompting. This is the student's instructional level.

- *Frustration:* The oral reading of the story is word-by-word and with much hesitation; there are a significant number of word recognition errors. During the retelling, even with *suggestive* and *specific* prompting, the student is not able to tell you much about the story. This is the student's frustration level.

Preparing Students for Individual Evaluation

Traditionally, reading instruction has required students to read a selection and then to answer questions as a way of developing and assessing comprehension. It seems reasonable to assume that the ability to make predictions and retell the story are usually not taught in most traditional reading programs. If this is true, and your students are in a traditional reading program, the teacher should either (a) use Form A: Subskills Format or (b) teach students how to predict and retell before administering Form B: Reader Response Format.

In most reading programs, reading evaluation tends to occur near the beginning of the school year. Therefore, it is recommended that before administering Form B: Reader Response Pretests and Posttests the teacher needs to model the predicting and retelling procedure with the whole class or with small groups.

What follows is a discussion of how to prepare students to make predictions and to retell stories in their own words. This will be followed by an example of how the teacher might actually model the procedure for students. It is believed that after the discussion and illustration of how to model the procedure for students, the teacher will be able to use Form B: Reader Response Pre-Post Testing for individual students.

Classroom Environment for Predicting and Retelling

Some students might not become involved easily in making predictions and retelling stories, even after the teacher models the procedure. If students are not sure of what to say or do, teachers may need to base their lessons on student experiences and social activities. The teacher should emphasize that a student's willingness to try is of utmost importance.

The teacher should consider the following:

- Develop themes or topics based on the age and interests of students; e.g., young students: animals or pets; older students: TV shows.
- Use a variety of instructional groupings: small groups, whole class or pairs.
- During this preparation period, students will need similar copies of stories and titles.
- During the predicting part, have students use only the title.

Steps in Predicting and Retelling Preparation Period

Predicting: (Allow approximately five minutes for predicting.)

Step 1   Use the title and ask the students to predict the plot or problem. Initially, ask them to work in pairs. Each pair of students can elect to write or discuss their responses. If they do write their responses, do not collect the papers.

Step 2   Ask the students to report their predictions. Record the predictions on the chalkboard, and discuss them. Predictions might be about plot, problem or words in the title. Tell students they will come back to their predictions after they have had an opportunity to hear the selection read by the teacher and have read it themselves.

Retelling: (Allow approximately ten minutes for retelling.)

Step 3   The students are to follow the selection as the teacher reads it aloud. After the teacher completes the selection, he should ask the students to read the selection silently. Again, it is more important for the student to understand the selection than it is for the student to memorize the selection.

Step 4   Go back to step one and discuss the various student predictions, not on the basis of whether they are correct or incorrect (good or bad) responses but rather on how "close" the predictions were or the "fun" of making predictions.

The previous steps merely outline the procedures used during prediction and retelling. What follows is an example of how to **introduce** these procedures in a lesson where the teacher is asked to **model** them for students.

Teacher as Model

Find a simple selection. The selection should have a title. The title must be large enough to be seen by the students.

Show the title. The teacher might make several predictions about what she **thinks the story or selection** will be about. Thus the teacher is modeling what the students are expected to do later.

Here is an example of a simple second-grade selection:

Find a picture of a bean seed (picture file or encyclopedia)

Title: *From Little Seed to Big Plants*

Predicting:	Teacher—"I think that this story is a real or true story. The picture shows a bean seed, and I know that seeds grow into plants. The story might be about how seeds grow into plants. That is my prediction or guess."
Selection:	(teacher reads aloud to the students) "What is in a seed?" asked Betty. Betty's brother gave her a big bean and said, "Cut this open and see." Betty cut the bean open. She found a baby plant in the bean. Betty asked her brother if another bean seed would grow if she planted it. Betty planted the seed and watered it every day. When Betty saw the leaves on the plant, she wanted to show them to everyone.
Retelling:	Teacher—"The main characters are Betty and her older brother. I think Betty was about seven years old. Her brother might have been in high school. (*Problem*) Betty wanted to know what was in a seed. This led Betty to actually grow the seed. I think Betty's brother helped her learn about seeds and how they grow. (*Outcome*) Betty saw the little plant in the seed. After she grew the seed, she learned that seeds grow into plants. I know that Betty was proud of her plant because she wanted to show everybody her new bean plant."

<u>Note:</u> The teacher never asked the students to predict or retell any part of the title or selection. The teacher did everything possible to **model** the procedure for the students.

The previous procedure is one way to prepare students for Form B: Reader Response Evaluation.

Summary of Specific Instructions—Form B: Reader Response Format

Step 1	The teacher needs to determine if the student understands the story/selection.
Step 2	If the student appears to have the ability to predict and retell the story, do not interrupt with prompting. Strive for a free flow of information.
Step 3	The questions used in the story guide at each grade level are merely suggestions. Feel free to modify or rephrase them.
Step 4	Take notes or use key words when the student is predicting and retelling on the Inventory Record Form.
Step 5	The teacher might like to tape record the student's responses to review the student's retelling at a later time.
Step 6	Once you become proficient in your ability to hear, prompt and score retellings, you may not always need to use the tape recorder. However, even when you become proficient, you may want to check your skills occasionally by using the tape recorder.

CRI SCORING AND INTERPRETATION

Form B: Pretest and Form B: Posttest

The following is a sample CRI record. This example is designed to enable the teacher to gain information on the scoring and interpretation of the Classroom Reading Inventory–Reader Response Format. The sample contains the following:

- A dialog for *getting started* with a student.
- Examples for scoring a student's responses.
- A sample Inventory Record–Reader Response Format for a second grader—Joan.
- A sample Inventory Record–Summary Sheet for Joan, to illustrate how to use and interpret Form B: Reader Response Format.

Getting Started Dialog:

Ms. Sage:	Joan, if I use words like *predict* or *prediction,* do you know what I mean?
Joan:	No.
Ms. Sage:	How about words like *guess* or *making guesses?*
Joan:	Yes, because I know how to guess.
Ms. Sage:	OK, let's practice making a guess. What do you think the cafeteria is having for lunch today?
Joan:	I don't know.
Ms. Sage:	OK, but you said you knew how to guess. How about making a guess? You don't have to be right. All you need to do is make a guess.
Joan:	I think they are having hamburgers.
Ms. Sage:	How will you actually know if they are having hamburgers?
Joan:	When I go to lunch.
Ms. Sage:	Joan, you made a good guess. Let's make more guesses now. I'm going to read you the **title of a story,** and I would like you to make guesses about what the story **might** be about.

Note: Since Joan is a second grader, the second-level selection *"Fish for Sale"* was selected as a place to start the testing.

Scoring a Student's Responses

The Inventory Record for Teachers directs the teacher to score student responses in the areas of Prediction: Title; Retelling: Character(s), Problem(s), and Outcome(s), on a scale of 1 – 2 – 3. On this scale a score of 1 is low, a score of 2 is average and a score of 3 is high.

Using Prediction as an example, the teacher would score the student as a 3 (high) if the student was able to predict the story content without any prompting. The teacher would score the student as a 2 (average) if the student was able to predict the story content with only some *general* prompting. The teacher would score the student as a 1 (low) if the student needed *suggestive* and *specific* prompting.

For the areas of Prediction: Title; Retelling: Character(s), Problem(s), and Outcome(s), the total scoring will be as follows:

TOTAL SCORE

10–12	comprehension excellent
6–9	comprehension needs assistance
5 or less	comprehension inadequate

Form B: Pretest Inventory Record
Summary Sheet

Student's Name: _____ _Joan_ _____ Grade: ___2___ Age: _7-6_

year, months

Date: _Today_ School: _____Troost_____ Administered by: ___J. White___

| Level | Predicting-Retelling | | | | | Reading Level | | |
	Prediction	Character(s)	Problem(s)	Outcome(s) Solution(s)	TOTAL	IND	INST	FRUST
1.								
2.	3	3	3	3	12	✓		
3.	3	1	1	1	6			✓
4.								
5.								
6.								
7.								
8.								

Summary of Responses:

Ability to Predict: _____Joan understands and is willing to make predictions._____

_____

_____

Ability to Retell: _____At the 2nd level, she appears to comprehend the selection._____

However, at the 3rd level, she needed help with characters, problems, and outcomes.

_____

Prompting to Obtain Predicting and Retelling Responses: _____Considerable prompting was needed_

at the 3rd level.

_____

Reading Level: _Joan is independent with 2nd-level material._____

Comments: _____Joan needs specific retelling practice. She appears to be a good reader for her_

_age and grade level._____

Form B: Pretest, Level 2

FISH FOR SALE

Susan got ten fish and a tank for her birthday. She loved the fish and learned to take good care of them.

One day Susan saw six new baby fish in the tank. The fish tank was too small for all of the fish. Dad said he would buy another tank for the baby fish.

Everyone began giving Susan fish and equipment. Soon she had tanks for big fish, small fish, and baby fish.

Each tank had water plants, air tubes, and stones on the bottom.

Mom said, "Enough! Susan, your room looks like a store for fish."

That gave Susan an idea. Why not put all of the fish tanks in the garage and put up a sign? Susan and her dad moved everything into the garage.

Susan made a big sign that read "FISH FOR SALE."

Student Responses

Low – High   (Circle number)
1   2   3

PREDICTION:
Title   1   2   ③
What do you think is meant by the title, "Fish for Sale"? What do you think the story will be about?

A kid wanted to buy a fish.

The fish are on sale.

RETELLING:

Character(s)   1   2   ③
What do you remember about the people in the story?

Susan got a fish for her birthday. The fish
had baby fish—six I think the story said.

Problem(s)   1   2   ③
What was the problem? What would you do if you had this problem?

Too many fish. Susan needed more tanks.
Susan's mother was upset. The room was
messy. I'd keep the room clean.

Outcome(s)/Solution(s)   1   2   ③
How was the problem solved? What do you think Susan's goal was?

Susan and her dad moved the fish tanks to
the garage. Susan got the idea to make a
sign and sell the fish.

SCORING GUIDE

TOTAL SCORE	_12_	Prompting		Reading Level	
10–12	Comprehension excellent	None	✓		
6–9	Comprehension needs assistance	General	____	IND	✓
5 or less	Comprehension inadequate	Specific	____	INST	____
		Suggestive	____	FRUST	____

Form B: Pretest, Level 3

SILLY BIRDS

With food all around them, baby turkeys will not eat. They don't know food when they see it. They often die for lack of water. Water is always kept in their bowls, but some of these birds never seem to discover what the water is for. We have a hard time trying to understand these silly birds.

Baby turkeys don't know enough to come out of the rain either. So many of the silly young birds catch cold and die. If they see anything bright, they will try to eat it. It may be a coin, a small nail, or even a shovel. You can see how foolish these silly birds are.

Student Responses

Low – High (Circle number)
1   2   3

PREDICTION:
Title   1   2   **(3)**
This story is about turkeys. Why do you think they are called silly birds?

Maybe because they do silly things like try
to run away.

RETELLING:
Character(s)   **(1)**   2   3
Can you tell me what the story said about turkeys?

That they were silly.

Problem(s)   **(1)**   2   3
What did the story say about turkeys eating and not eating?

That they would not eat (why not?).
They weren't hungry.

Outcome(s)/Solution(s) **(1)**   2   3
Can you tell me what happens to turkeys when they do silly things?

They don't get anything to eat.

SCORING GUIDE

TOTAL SCORE   _6_

		Prompting		Reading Level	
10–12	Comprehension excellent	None	___		
(6–9)	Comprehension needs assistance	General	___	IND	___
5 or less	Comprehension inadequate	Specific	✓	INST	___
		Suggestive	✓	FRUST	✓

Summary of Specific Instructions

Step 1   Establish rapport. Don't be in a hurry to begin testing. Put the student at ease. Make her feel comfortable.

Step 2   Begin at the level of the student's current grade level. If, for example, the student is a third grader, begin with a third-grade selection. If the student has the ability to predict and retell, and is reading comfortably, go to the fourth-grade-level selection. If the student is having difficulty, drop back to the second-grade-level selection. If you have reason to believe that the student is reading above or below grade level, adjust the starting level accordingly.

Step 3   Read the title aloud. Take care to cover the selection while reading. Using the title, ask the student to predict, to make guesses about the selection. If necessary, use a prompting strategy.

Step 4   Have the student read the selection aloud to you. After reading, ask the student to retell the story by noting character(s), problem(s), and outcome(s)/solution(s). The guided questions listed for the predicting and retelling scorable areas are merely suggestions. Feel free to change them as desired.

Step 5   If it becomes necessary to prompt, use a *general* prompt first so as to not give the story away. If the student needs *suggestive* or *specific* prompting, it is safe to assume that the student is having difficulty comprehending what he is reading.

Step 6   As previously stated, the independent reading level is the level at which the student is able to read without difficulty; i.e., the oral reading of the story is fluent and expressive; there are few if any significant word recognition errors. During the retelling, the student has no difficulty in recalling the character(s), the problem(s), and the outcome(s)/solution(s).

Step 7   Transfer the independent reading level and the scorable parts total to the Inventory Record–Summary Sheet.

READER RESPONSE FORMAT
FORM B: PRETEST

Graded Paragraphs

IT'S MY BALL

Tom and Nancy went for a walk.

They saw a small ball on the grass.

They began fighting over the ball.

While they were fighting, a dog picked up the ball and ran.

The kids ran after the dog, but the dog got away.

FISH FOR SALE

Susan got ten fish and a tank for her birthday.

She loved the fish and learned to take good care of them.

One day, Susan saw six new baby fish in the tank.

The fish tank was too small for all of the fish.

Dad said he would buy another tank for the baby fish.

Everyone began giving Susan fish and equipment.

Soon she had tanks for big fish, small fish, and baby fish.

Each tank had water plants, air tubes, and stones on the bottom.

Mom said, "Enough! Susan, your room looks like a store for fish."

That gave Susan an idea. Why not put all of the fish tanks in the garage and

put up a sign?

Susan and her dad moved everything into the garage.

Susan made a big sign that read "FISH FOR SALE."

SILLY BIRDS

With food all around them, baby turkeys will not eat. They don't know food when they see it. They often die for lack of water. Water is always kept in their bowls, but some of these birds never seem to discover what the water is for. We have a hard time trying to understand these silly birds.

Baby turkeys don't know enough to come out of the rain either. So many of the silly young birds catch cold and die. If they see anything bright, they will try to eat it. It may be a coin, a small nail, or even a shovel. You can see how foolish these silly birds are.

ONE OF A KIND

"We found one," Kate whispered to her brother as they discover a deep burrow on the side of the pond. They had found a home of a platypus.

Tom and Kate are from Australia. So is the platypus. This brother and sister have studied the platypus since they were children. These animals look a lot like ducks with fur. They are one of only two mammals in the world that lays eggs.

They live in the water and on land. They waddle when they walk. However, they swim sleekly and smoothly. The animals dive to find food on the bottom of streams, lakes and ponds. They have soft rubbery bills.

Platypuses find their prey using special detectors inside their bills. These detectors sense the tiny movements of their prey. Sharks are another water animal with these special detectors inside their mouths.

Platypus are only active at night. Tom and Kate wait in silence to watch for the platypus long after the sun has set. They see a platypus under the water swinging her head from side to side trying to find a meal.

THE FOX—A FARMER'S BEST FRIEND

"Meg, look! That's a female fox ready to have cubs." Uncle Mike was excited. "I haven't seen a fox around here for ten years." Meg said, "Shall I get your gun?" "There's no need for a gun," Uncle Mike replied. "Foxes help farmers by eating pests like mice, squirrels, frogs, and insects."

The next day Meg and her uncle were unhappy to learn that some farmers were hunting for the fox. These farmers didn't believe that a fox was helpful. Foxes save the farmers' crops by eating pests that destroy their crops. The farmers were sure that foxes only killed chickens and other small animals.

After weeks of hunting, the farmers gave up trying to kill the fox. When Uncle Mike and Meg found fresh fox and cub tracks on the far end of their farm, they were pleased the fox had not been killed.

HUSH MY BABY

Nate was a slave who lived with his master in Baltimore. Nate wanted freedom. He got an idea. "What if I build a big box, big enough so I could hide in it?" Nate got busy, and when the box was built, he got inside of it. Nate's uncle put the box on a ship that was going to New York. It was very cold in the box. Nate was afraid he would not make it to freedom.

On a Sunday morning, the ship arrived in New York. Nate's friend John was waiting at the dock. The ship's captain told John they didn't deliver boxes on Sunday. John worried that Nate might die from being in the box too long. He talked the captain into letting him take the box with him.

While the captain was helping John load the box onto a wagon, Nate sneezed. John was afraid that Nate would be discovered and sent back to his owner. To cover the noise of Nate's sneeze, John started singing "Hush My Baby." This also warned Nate to be very quiet. At last the box was delivered to the right house. It was opened, and out popped Nate, cold and stiff—but happy and free!

THE HURT OF SHAME

Sticks and stones can break my bones, but words can never hurt me. Is this old rhyme true?

We all want people to see us as talented and special in some way. There are times we cannot be this ideal picture of ourselves or always be at our best. When those around us take notice, we can feel the hurt of shame.

This happens especially when we are blocked from something we want and enjoy, like friends and acceptance by others. It also can happen when we are thwarted from exciting or pleasing activities, such as making the sports team or being in the school band. We feel shame when our looks, clothes or achievements appear as being less.

In most cases, a broken bone can be healed, but not always a broken heart. Experiences of shame and their memory can hurt for a lifetime. The next time you see someone bullied or shamed, try to recall hurt feelings you yourself have experienced. Feel care and support for the victim. Helping people maintain their dignity and self respect helps heal the hurt of shame.

THE WORLD OF DINOSAURS

Before the 1800s, no one knew that dinosaurs had ever existed. Once in a while, people would find a dinosaur tooth or bone but did not realize what it was.

When dinosaurs lived, the earth was not like it is today. Mountains like the Alps, for example, had not yet been formed.

The first dinosaur appeared on the earth about 220 million years ago. For 150 million years or so, they ruled the earth. Suddenly, about 63 million years ago, dinosaurs died out.

What caused this "terrible lizard," for that is what *dinosaur* means in English, to die out so suddenly?

Scientists have developed lots of theories to try to explain what happened to the dinosaurs. One theory is that the earth became too cold for them.

Most scientists believe that no single theory explains what happened to the dinosaurs. It may be that they could not keep up with the way the earth was changing. Whatever the cause, or causes, it was the end of the World of Dinosaurs.

READER RESPONSE FORMAT
FORM B: PRETEST

Inventory Record for Teachers

Form B: Pretest Inventory Record
Summary Sheet

Student's Name: _____ **Grade:** _____ **Age:** _____
year, months

Date: _____ **School:** _____ **Administered by:** _____

	Predicting-Retelling					Reading Level		
Level	Prediction	Character(s)	Problem(s)	Outcome(s) Solution(s)	TOTAL	IND	INST	FRUST
1.								
2.								
3.								
4.								
5.								
6.								
7.								
8.								

Summary of Responses:

Ability to Predict: _____

_____

_____

Ability to Retell: _____

_____

_____

Prompting to Obtain Predicting and Retelling Responses: _____

_____

_____

Reading Level: _____

Comments: _____

_____

Form B: Pretest, Level 1

IT'S MY BALL

Tom and Nancy went for a walk.

They saw a small ball on the grass.

They began fighting over the ball.

While they were fighting, a dog picked up the ball

and ran.

The kids ran after the dog, but the dog got away.

Student Responses

Low	–	High	(Circle number)
1	2	3	

PREDICTION:
Title   1   2   3
What do you think the story will be about?

_____

_____

_____

RETELLING:

Character(s)   1   2   3
What do you remember about the people in the story?

_____

_____

_____

Problem(s)   1   2   3
What was the problem? If you were in that situation, what would you do?

_____

_____

_____

Outcome(s)/Solution(s) 1   2   3
How was the problem solved?

_____

_____

_____

SCORING GUIDE

TOTAL SCORE _____

		Prompting		Reading Level	
10–12	Comprehension excellent	None	_____		
6–9	Comprehension needs assistance	General	_____	IND	_____
5 or less	Comprehension inadequate	Specific	_____	INST	_____
		Suggestive	_____	FRUST	_____

Form B: Pretest, Level 2

FISH FOR SALE

Susan got ten fish and a tank for her birthday. She loved the fish and learned to take good care of them.

One day, Susan saw six new baby fish in the tank. The fish tank was too small for all of the fish. Dad said he would buy another tank for the baby fish.

Everyone began giving Susan fish and equipment. Soon she had tanks for big fish, small fish, and baby fish.

Each tank had water plants, air tubes, and stones on the bottom.

Mom said, "Enough! Susan, your room looks like a store for fish."

That gave Susan an idea. Why not put all of the fish tanks in the garage and put up a sign?

Susan and her dad moved everything into the garage.

Susan made a big sign that read, "FISH FOR SALE."

Student Responses

Low   –   High   (Circle number)
1   2   3

PREDICTION:
Title   1   2   3
What do you think is meant by the title "Fish for Sale"? What do you think the story will be about?

_____
_____
_____

RETELLING:
Character(s)   1   2   3
What do you remember about the people in the story?

_____
_____
_____

Problem(s)   1   2   3
What was the problem? What would you do if you had this problem?

_____
_____
_____

Outcome(s)/Solution(s) 1   2   3
How was the problem solved? What do you think Susan's goal was?

_____
_____
_____

SCORING GUIDE

TOTAL SCORE _____		Prompting		Reading Level	
10–12	Comprehension excellent	None	_____		
6–9	Comprehension needs assistance	General	_____	IND	_____
5 or less	Comprehension inadequate	Specific	_____	INST	_____
		Suggestive	_____	FRUST	_____

Form B: Pretest, Level 3

SILLY BIRDS

With food all around them, baby turkeys will not eat. They don't know food when they see it. They often die for lack of water. Water is always kept in their bowls, but some of these birds never seem to discover what the water is for. We have a hard time trying to understand these silly birds.

Baby turkeys don't know enough to come out of the rain either. So many of the silly young birds catch cold and die. If they see anything bright, they will try to eat it. It may be a coin, a small nail, or even a shovel. You can see how foolish these silly birds are.

Student Responses

Low – High   (Circle number)
1   2   3

PREDICTION:
Title   1   2   3
This story is about turkeys. Why do you think they are called silly birds?

_____

_____

_____

RETELLING:
Character(s)   1   2   3
Can you tell me what the story said about turkeys?

_____

_____

_____

Problem(s)   1   2   3
What did the story say about turkeys eating and not eating?

_____

_____

_____

Outcome(s)/Solution(s) 1   2   3
Can you tell me what happens to turkeys when they do silly things?

_____

_____

_____

SCORING GUIDE

TOTAL SCORE _____		Prompting		Reading Level	
10–12	Comprehension excellent	None	_____		
6–9	Comprehension needs assistance	General	_____	IND	_____
5 or less	Comprehension inadequate	Specific	_____	INST	_____
		Suggestive	_____	FRUST	_____

Form B: Pretest, Level 4

ONE OF A KIND

"We found one," Kate whispered to her brother as they discover a deep burrow on the side of the pond. They had found a home of a platypus.

Tom and Kate are from Australia. So is the platypus. They have studied the platypus since they were children. These animals look a lot like ducks with fur. They are one of two mammals in the world that lays eggs.

Active at night, they live in the water and on land. They waddle when they walk, but they swim sleekly and smoothly. The animals dive for food on the bottom of streams, lakes and ponds. They have soft rubbery bills.

Platypuses find their prey using special detectors inside their bills. These detectors sense the tiny movements of their prey. Sharks are another water animal with these special detectors inside their mouths.

Tom and Kate wait in silence to watch for the platypus long after the sun has set. They see a platypus under the water swinging her head from side to side trying to find a meal.

Student Responses

Low   –   High   (Circle number)
1   2   3

PREDICTION:
Title   1   2   3
Why was the story titled "One of a Kind"?

_____

_____

_____

RETELLING:
Character(s)   1   2   3
What can you tell me about the platypus?

_____

_____

_____

Problem(s)   1   2   3
How do the platypuses live?

_____

_____

_____

Outcome(s)/Solution(s)   1   2   3
Why do you think Tom and Kate want to study the platypus?

_____

_____

_____

SCORING GUIDE

TOTAL SCORE _____		Promoting		Reading Level	
10–12	Comprehension excellent	None	_____		
6–9	Comprehension needs assistance	General	_____	IND	_____
5 or less	Comprehension inadequate	Specific	_____	INST	_____
		Suggestive	_____	FRUST	_____

Form B: Pretest, Level 5

THE FOX—A FARMER'S BEST FRIEND

"Meg, look! That's a female fox ready to have cubs." Uncle Mike was excited. "I haven't seen a fox around here for ten years." Meg said, "Shall I get your gun?" "There's no need for a gun," Uncle Mike replied. "Foxes help farmers by eating pests like mice, squirrels, frogs, and insects."

The next day Meg and her uncle were unhappy to learn that some farmers were hunting for the fox. These farmers didn't believe that a fox was helpful. Foxes save the farmers' crops by eating pests that destroy their crops. The farmers were sure that foxes only killed chickens and other small animals.

After weeks of hunting, the farmers gave up trying to kill the fox. When Uncle Mike and Meg found fresh fox and cub tracks on the far end of their farm, they were pleased the fox had not been killed.

Student Responses

Low – High   (Circle number)
1   2   3

PREDICTION:
Title   1   2   3
Have you ever seen a fox? If not, discuss things about a fox. What do you think the story will be about?

_____

_____

_____

RETELLING:
Character(s)   1   2   3
What can you tell me about the people in the story?

_____

_____

_____

Problem(s)   1   2   3
The fox had a problem. What do you think was happening? Why do you think Meg and Uncle Mike worried?

_____

_____

Outcome(s)/Solution(s) 1   2   3
What happened to the fox? When Uncle Mike and Meg saw the tracks, what did they learn? How did Uncle Mike and Meg feel?

_____

_____

_____

SCORING GUIDE

TOTAL SCORE _____		Prompting		Reading Level	
10–12	Comprehension excellent	None	_____		
6–9	Comprehension needs assistance	General	_____	IND	_____
5 or less	Comprehension inadequate	Specific	_____	INST	_____
		Suggestive	_____	FRUST	_____

Form B: Pretest, Level 6

HUSH MY BABY

Nate was a slave who lived with his master in Baltimore. Nate wanted freedom. He got an idea. "What if I build a big box, big enough so I could hide in it?" Nate got busy, and when the box was built, he got inside of it. Nate's uncle put the box on a ship that was going to New York. It was very cold in the box. Nate was afraid he would not make it to freedom.

On a Sunday morning, the ship arrived in New York. Nate's friend John was waiting at the dock. The ship's captain told John they didn't deliver boxes on Sunday. John worried that Nate might die from being in the box too long. He talked the captain into letting him take the box with him.

While the captain was helping John load the box onto a wagon, Nate sneezed. John was afraid that Nate would be discovered and sent back to his owner. To cover the noise of Nate's sneeze, John started singing "Hush My Baby." This also warned Nate to be very quiet. At last the box was delivered to the right house. It was opened, and out popped Nate, cold and stiff—but happy and free!

Student Responses

Low – High   (Circle number)
1   2   3

PREDICTION:
Title   1   2   3
This is a story about a slave. What can you tell me about slaves?

_____

_____

RETELLING:
Character(s)   1   2   3
Who was Nate and what did he want to do?

_____

_____

Problem(s)   1   2   3
What problem did Nate try to solve?

_____

_____

Outcome(s)/Solution(s) 1   2   3
What happened to Nate?

_____

_____

_____

SCORING GUIDE

TOTAL SCORE _____

		Prompting		Reading Level	
10–12	Comprehension excellent	None	_____		
6–9	Comprehension needs assistance	General	_____	IND	_____
5 or less	Comprehension inadequate	Specific	_____	INST	_____
		Suggestive	_____	FRUST	_____

Form B: Pretest, Level 7

THE HURT OF SHAME

Sticks and stones can break my bones, but words can never hurt me. Is this old rhyme true?

We all want people to see us as talented and special in some way. There are times we cannot be this ideal picture of ourselves or always be at our best. When those around us take notice, we can feel the hurt of shame.

This happens especially when we are blocked from something we want and enjoy, like friends and acceptance by others. It also can happen when we are thwarted from exciting or pleasing activities, such as making the sports team or being in the school band. We feel shame when our looks, clothes or achievements appear as being less.

In most cases, a broken bone can be healed, but not always a broken heart. Experiences of shame and their memory can hurt for a lifetime. The next time you see someone bullied or shamed, try to recall hurt feelings you yourself have experienced. Feel care and support for the victim. Helping people maintain their dignity and self respect helps heal the hurt of shame.

Student Responses

Low   –   High   (Circle number)
1   2   3

PREDICTION:
Title   1   2   3
What is the hurt of shame?

_____

_____

_____

RETELLING:
Character(s)   1   2   3
What are times we might feel shame?

_____

_____

Problem(s)   1   2   3
What is the problem with shame? How would you handle this problem?

_____

_____

Outcome(s)/Solution(s)   1   2   3
What heals the hurt of shame?

_____

_____

_____

SCORING GUIDE

TOTAL SCORE _____		Promoting		Reading Level	
10–12	Comprehension excellent	None	_____		
6–9	Comprehension needs assistance	General	_____	IND	_____
5 or less	Comprehension inadequate	Specific	_____	INST	_____
		Suggestive	_____	FRUST	_____

Form B: Pretest, Level 8

THE WORLD OF DINOSAURS

Before the 1800s, no one knew that dinosaurs had ever existed. Once in a while, people would find a dinosaur tooth or bone but did not realize what it was.

When dinosaurs lived, the earth was not like it is today. Mountains like the Alps, for example, had not yet been formed.

The first dinosaur appeared on the earth about 220 million years ago. For 150 million years or so, they ruled the earth. Suddenly, about 63 million years ago, dinosaurs died out.

What caused this "terrible lizard," for that is what *dinosaur* means in English, to die out so suddenly?

Scientists have developed lots of theories to try to explain what happened to the dinosaurs. One theory is that the earth became too cold for them.

Most scientists believe that no single theory explains what happened to the dinosaurs. It may be that they could not keep up with the way the earth was changing. Whatever the cause, or causes, it was the end of the World of Dinosaurs.

Student Responses

Low – High   (Circle number)
1   2   3

PREDICTION:
Title   1   2   3
What can you tell me about dinosaurs?

_____
_____
_____

RETELLING:
Character(s)   1   2   3
Tell me what you can about dinosaurs.

_____
_____
_____

Problem(s)   1   2   3
What problem did the dinosaurs have with their environment?

_____
_____
_____

Outcome(s)/Solution(s) 1   2   3
What happened to the dinosaurs?

_____
_____
_____

SCORING GUIDE

TOTAL SCORE _____		Prompting		Reading Level	
10–12	Comprehension excellent	None	_____		
6–9	Comprehension needs assistance	General	_____	IND	_____
5 or less	Comprehension inadequate	Specific	_____	INST	_____
		Suggestive	_____	FRUST	_____

READER RESPONSE FORMAT
FORM B: POSTTEST

Graded Paragraphs

THE RED ANT

The red ant lives under the sand.

The ant must build its own room.

It has to take the sand outside.

The sand is made into little hills.

Building a room is hard work.

The red ant is a busy bug.

WHY CAN'T I PLAY?

Kim wanted to play on the boys' team.

The boys said, "No."

One day the boys needed one more player.

They asked Kim to play.

Kim got the ball and kicked it a long way.

She was a fast runner and a good player.

Todd, a boy on the team, kicked the ball to her.

Kim kicked the ball down the side of the field.

Tony, a boy on the other team, tried to block her.

He missed, and Kim scored.

Someone said, "Kim should have played on the team all year."

FLOODS ARE DANGEROUS

Mrs. Sánchez was driving home with her two sons, Luis and Ernesto. From the darkening sky, Mrs. Sánchez could see that a storm was coming. Soon, lightning flashed, thunder boomed, and the rain poured down. In order to get to her house, Mrs. Sánchez had to cross a road covered with water. She decided to drive across the rushing water. When they were just about across the road, the rising water caused the car to float away. Mrs. Sánchez knew that she had to get the boys and herself out of that car.

Luis was able to roll down the window and jump to dry ground. Mrs. Sánchez also jumped to dry ground. Mrs. Sánchez and Luis tried to grab Ernesto, but the car floated out of reach.

Soon the police and some friends came, and they searched all night for Ernesto and the car. They were unable to find them. Had Ernesto drowned in the flood, or was he safe?

Early the next day, Mrs. Sánchez saw a police car drive up to her house. Her heart raced when she saw Ernesto in the police car. He was safe! Ernesto told his mother that their car got stuck against a tree and that he was able to climb out of the car. He sat in the tree until daylight when the police found him. Everyone was happy to see Ernesto again.

FIRST TO DIE

It was very cold that March day in Boston. The year was 1770. It was a time of protest and riots. The people of Boston had had it with British rule.

Nobody knew that the day would end in bloodshed. This was the day of the Boston Massacre—March 5, 1770.

Somewhere in the city that night, a black man and former slave named Crispus Attucks was moving toward his place in history.

The British had brought troops into Boston in 1768. There were fights between the people of Boston and the soldiers.

On the night of March 6, 1770, the streets were filled with men. They were angry. Crispus Attucks was the leader of a patriot crowd of men. They met up with a group of British soldiers. The crowd pushed in on the soldiers. There was much confusion. A soldier fired his rifle. Attucks fell into the gutter—dead.

Crispus Attucks had been a leader in the night's actions. A black man and a former slave, he had helped to bring about action that led to the foundation of American independence.

TIGER

Tiger is hungry. He has not eaten for five days. His last meal was a wild pig. It is dark now, and Tiger is on a hunt. As he slinks through the jungle, the muscles of his powerful neck and shoulders are tense. Tiger senses that there are humans close by. Tiger is careful to avoid humans. He knows that only old or sick tigers will hunt humans because they are no longer swift enough to hunt other animals.

Suddenly, Tiger's sensitive nostrils pick up the scent of an animal. Tiger creeps slowly toward the smell. There, in a clearing in the jungle, he sees a goat. The goat has picked up Tiger's scent. Tiger moves in, but the goat does not flee. It is a trap! Humans have tied the goat there to trap Tiger. Tiger stops, then moves back into the jungle.

Tiger is hungry.

SENTINELS IN THE FOREST

Many wild creatures that travel with their own kind know by instinct how to protect the group. One of them acts as a sentinel.

Hidden by the branches of a low-hanging tree, I once watched two white-tailed deer feeding in a meadow. At first, my interest was held by their beauty. But soon I noticed something strange; they were taking turns feeding. While one was calmly cropping grass, unafraid and at ease, the other—with head high, eyes sweeping the sea marsh, and sensitive nostrils "feeling" the air—stood on guard against enemies. Not for a moment, during the half hour I spied upon them, did they stop their teamwork.

I LOVE A MYSTERY

Ever since the year 1841, when Edgar Allan Poe wrote *The Murders in the Rue Morgue,* people around the world have become fans of the mystery/detective story.

The mystery begins with a strange crime. There are a number of clues. A detective is called in to solve the mysterious crime. The clues may lead the detective to or away from the solution. In the end the detective reveals the criminal and tells how the mystery was solved.

The detective in most mystery stories is usually not a regular police officer, but a private detective. Probably the most famous of all these private detectives is Sherlock Holmes. With his friend and assistant Dr. Watson, Sherlock Holmes solved many strange crimes.

One of the most popular of all the mysteries that Holmes solved is called *The Hound of the Baskervilles.* In this story a man is murdered, and the only clue Holmes has to go on is an enormous hound's footprints found next to the dead man's body.

Do you love a mystery?

IT CANNOT BE HELPED

There is a phrase the Japanese use when something difficult must be endured—*it cannot be helped.*

On a quiet Sunday morning in early December 1941, the Japanese launched a surprise attack on Pearl Harbor. Shortly after that, the Army and the FBI began arresting all Japanese who were living along the West Coast of the United States. Every Japanese man, woman, and child, 110,000 of them, was sent to inland prison camps. Even though the Japanese had been living in the United States since 1869, they were never allowed to become citizens. Suddenly, they were a people with no rights who looked exactly like the enemy.

With the closing of the prison camps in the fall of 1945, the families were sent back to the West Coast.

The Japanese relocation program, carried through at such great cost in misery and tragedy, was justified on the ground that the Japanese were potentially disloyal. However the record does not show a single case of Japanese disloyalty or sabotage during the whole war.

In June 1952, Congress passed Public Law 414, granting Japanese the right to become United States citizens.

READER RESPONSE FORMAT
FORM B: POSTTEST

Inventory Record for Teachers

Form B: Posttest Inventory Record
Summary Sheet

Student's Name: _____ Grade: _____ Age: _____

year, months

Date: _____ School: _____ Administered by: _____

	Predicting-Retelling					Reading Level		
Level	Prediction	Character(s)	Problem(s)	Outcome(s) Solution(s)	TOTAL	IND	INST	FRUST
1.								
2.								
3.								
4.								
5.								
6.								
7.								
8.								

Summary of Responses:

Ability to Predict: _____

_____

_____

Ability to Retell: _____

_____

_____

Prompting to Obtain Predicting and Retelling Responses: _____

_____

_____

Reading Level: _____

Comments: _____

_____

Form B: Posttest, Level 1

THE RED ANT

The red ant lives under the sand.

The ant must build its own room.

It has to take the sand outside.

The sand is made into little hills.

Building a room is hard work.

The red ant is a busy bug.

Student Responses

Low – High   (Circle number)
1   2   3

PREDICTION:
Title   1   2   3
What do you think the story will be about?
_____
_____
_____

RETELLING:
Character(s)   1   2   3
What can you tell me about the red ant?
_____
_____
_____

Problem(s)   1   2   3
What did the red ant have to do to build its room?
_____
_____
_____

Outcome(s)/Solution(s) 1   2   3
What can you tell me about the red ant's work habits?
_____
_____
_____

SCORING GUIDE

TOTAL SCORE _____		Prompting		Reading Level	
10–12	Comprehension excellent	None	_____		
6–9	Comprehension needs assistance	General	_____	IND	_____
5 or less	Comprehension inadequate	Specific	_____	INST	_____
		Suggestive	_____	FRUST	_____

Form B: Posttest, Level 2

WHY CAN'T I PLAY?

Kim wanted to play on the boys' team.

The boys said, "No."

One day, the boys needed one more player.

They asked Kim to play.

Kim got the ball and kicked it a long way.

She was a fast runner and a good player.

Todd, a boy on the team, kicked the ball to her.

Kim kicked the ball down the side of the field.

Tony, a boy on the other team, tried to block her.

He missed, and Kim scored.

Someone said, "Kim should have played on the

team all year."

Student Responses

Low   –   High   (Circle number)
1   2   3

PREDICTION:
Title   1   2   3
What do you think is meant by the title "Why Can't I Play?" What do you think the story will be about?

_____

_____

RETELLING:
Character(s)   1   2   3
Who was the main person in the story? Can you tell me more about that person?

_____

_____

_____

Problem(s)   1   2   3
What was the problem? Can you tell me anything more?

_____

_____

_____

Outcome(s)/Solution(s) 1   2   3
How was the problem solved?

_____

_____

_____

SCORING GUIDE

TOTAL SCORE _____		Prompting		Reading Level	
10–12	Comprehension excellent	None	_____		
6–9	Comprehension needs assistance	General	_____	IND	_____
5 or less	Comprehension inadequate	Specific	_____	INST	_____
		Suggestive	_____	FRUST	_____

Form B: Posttest, Level 3

FLOODS ARE DANGEROUS

Mrs. Sanchez was driving home with her two sons, Luis and Ernesto. From the darkening sky, Mrs. Sanchez could see that a storm was coming. Soon, lightning flashed, thunder boomed, and the rain poured down. In order to get to her house, Mrs. Sanchez had to cross a road covered with water. She decided to drive across the rushing water. When they were just about across the road, the rising water caused the car to float away. Mrs. Sanchez knew that she had to get the boys and herself out of that car.

Luis was able to roll down the window and jump to dry ground. Mrs. Sanchez also jumped to dry ground. Mrs. Sanchez and Luis tried to grab Ernesto, but the car floated out of reach.

Soon the police and some friends came, and they searched all night for Ernesto and the car. They were unable to find them. Had Ernesto drowned in the flood, or was he safe?

Early the next day, Mrs. Sanchez saw a police car drive up to her house. Her heart raced when she saw Ernesto in the police car. He was safe! Ernesto told his mother that their car got stuck against a tree and that he was able to climb out of the car. He sat in the tree until daylight when the police found him. Everyone was happy to see Ernesto again.

Student Responses

Low   –   High   (Circle number)
1   2   3

PREDICTION:
Title   1   2   3
What do you think can happen if a car tries to cross a road that is flooded?

_____

_____

RETELLING:
Character(s)   1   2   3
What do you remember about the people in the story? How do you think they felt?

_____

_____

Problem(s)   1   2   3
What was the problem? What do you think caused the problem?

_____

_____

Outcome(s)/Solution(s)   1   2   3
How do you think the problem was solved? How do you think you would feel in this situation?

_____

_____

_____

SCORING GUIDE

TOTAL SCORE _____		Prompting		Reading Level	
10–12	Comprehension excellent	None	_____		
6–9	Comprehension needs assistance	General	_____	IND	_____
5 or less	Comprehension inadequate	Specific	_____	INST	_____
		Suggestive	_____	FRUST	_____

Form B: Posttest, Level 4

FIRST TO DIE

It was very cold that March day in Boston. The year was 1770. It was a time of protest and riots. The people of Boston had had it with British rule.

Nobody knew that the day would end in bloodshed. This was the day of the Boston Massacre—March 5, 1770.

Somewhere in the city that night, a black man and former slave named Crispus Attucks was moving toward his place in history.

The British had brought troops into Boston in 1768. There were fights between the people of Boston and the soldiers.

On the night of March 6, 1770, the streets were filled with men. They were angry. Crispus Attucks was the leader of a patriot crowd of men. They met up with a group of British soldiers. The crowd pushed in on the soldiers. There was much confusion. A soldier fired his rifle. Attucks fell into the gutter—dead.

Crispus Attucks had been a leader in the night's actions. A black man and a former slave, he had helped to bring about action that led to the foundation of American independence.

Student Responses

Low – High   (Circle number)
1   2   3

PREDICTION:
Title   1   2   3
This story is about a man named Crispus Attucks. What do you think happened to him?

_____

_____

_____

RETELLING:
Character(s)   1   2   3
What can you tell me about Crispus Attucks?

_____

_____

Problem(s)   1   2   3
What was the problem between the British soldiers and the people of Boston?

_____

_____

_____

Outcome(s)/Solution(s) 1   2   3
What happened to Attucks? What was the result of what he did?

_____

_____

_____

SCORING GUIDE

TOTAL SCORE	_____	Prompting		Reading Level	
10–12	Comprehension excellent	None	_____		
6–9	Comprehension needs assistance	General	_____	IND	_____
5 or less	Comprehension inadequate	Specific	_____	INST	_____
		Suggestive	_____	FRUST	_____

Form B: Posttest, Level 5

TIGER

Tiger is hungry. He has not eaten for five days. His last meal was a wild pig. It is dark now, and Tiger is on a hunt. As he slinks through the jungle, the muscles of his powerful neck and shoulders are tense. Tiger senses that there are humans close by. Tiger is careful to avoid humans. He knows that only old or sick tigers will hunt humans because they are no longer swift enough to hunt other animals.

Suddenly, Tiger's sensitive nostrils pick up the scent of an animal. Tiger creeps slowly toward the smell. There, in a clearing in the jungle, he sees a goat. The goat has picked up Tiger's scent. Tiger moves in, but the goat does not flee. It is a trap! Humans have tied the goat there to trap Tiger. Tiger stops, then moves back into the jungle.

Tiger is hungry.

Student Responses

Low   –   High   (Circle number)
1   2   3

PREDICTION:
Title   1   2   3
Have you ever seen a tiger? What can you tell me about tigers?

_____

_____

_____

RETELLING:
Character(s)   1   2   3
Tell me what happened to Tiger in this story.

_____

_____

_____

Problem(s)   1   2   3
Tiger had a problem. What was it? What did he do?

_____

_____

_____

Outcome(s)/Solution(s) 1   2   3
What happened to Tiger? Why wasn't Tiger trapped?

_____

_____

_____

SCORING GUIDE

TOTAL SCORE	_____	Prompting		Reading Level	
10–12	Comprehension excellent	None	_____		
6–9	Comprehension needs assistance	General	_____	IND	_____
5 or less	Comprehension inadequate	Specific	_____	INST	_____
		Suggestive	_____	FRUST	_____

Form B: Posttest, Level 6

SENTINELS IN THE FOREST

Many wild creatures that travel with their own kind know by instinct how to protect the group. One of them acts as a sentinel.

Hidden by the branches of a low-hanging tree, I once watched two white-tailed deer feeding in a meadow. At first, my interest was held by their beauty. But soon I noticed something strange; they were taking turns feeding. While one was calmly cropping grass, unafraid and at ease, the other—with head high, eyes sweeping the sea marsh, and sensitive nostrils "feeling" the air— stood on guard against enemies. Not for a moment, during the half hour I spied upon them, did they stop their teamwork.

Student Responses

Low   –   High   (Circle number)
1   2   3

PREDICTION:
Title   1   2   3
What will this story be about?

_____

_____

_____

RETELLING:
Character(s)   1   2   3
This story is not about a person. Can you tell about the animals in the story?

_____

_____

_____

Problem(s)   1   2   3
Tell about what the animals were doing.

_____

_____

_____

Outcome(s)/Solution(s) 1   2   3
Do you think the animals were good at what they were doing? Tell me more about it.

_____

_____

_____

SCORING GUIDE

TOTAL SCORE _____		Prompting		Reading Level	
10–12	Comprehension excellent	None	_____		
6–9	Comprehension needs assistance	General	_____	IND	_____
5 or less	Comprehension inadequate	Specific	_____	INST	_____
		Suggestive	_____	FRUST	_____

Form B: Posttest, Level 7

I LOVE A MYSTERY

Ever since the year 1841, when Edgar Allan Poe wrote *The Murders in the Rue Morgue*, people around the world have become fans of the mystery/detective story.

The mystery begins with a strange crime. There are a number of clues. A detective is called in to solve the mysterious crime. The clues may lead the detective to or away from the solution. In the end the detective reveals the criminal and tells how the mystery was solved.

The detective in most mystery stories is usually not a regular police officer but a private detective. Probably the most famous of all these private detectives is Sherlock Holmes. With his friend and assistant Dr. Watson, Sherlock Holmes solved many strange crimes.

One of the most popular of all the mysteries that Holmes solved is called *The Hound of the Baskervilles*. In this story a man is murdered, and the only clue Holmes has to go on is an enormous hound's footprints found next to the dead man's body.

Do you love a mystery?

Student Responses

Low   –   High   (Circle number)
1   2   3

PREDICTION:
Title   1   2   3
Tell me why you think this story is called "I Love a Mystery."

_____

_____

_____

RETELLING:
Character(s)   1   2   3
What kind of a person is this story about?

_____

_____

_____

Problem(s)   1   2   3
What problems do these people have?

_____

_____

_____

Outcome(s)/Solution(s) 1   2   3
How do they do what they do?

_____

_____

_____

SCORING GUIDE

TOTAL SCORE _____	Prompting		Reading Level	
10–12 Comprehension excellent	None	_____		
6–9 Comprehension needs assistance	General	_____	IND	_____
5 or less Comprehension inadequate	Specific	_____	INST	_____
	Suggestive	_____	FRUST	_____

Form B: Posttest, Level 8

IT CANNOT BE HELPED

There is a phrase the Japanese use when something difficult must be endured—*it cannot be helped*.

On a quiet Sunday morning in early December of 1941, the Japanese launched a surprise attack on Pearl Harbor. Shortly after that, the Army and the FBI began arresting all Japanese who were living along the West Coast of the United States. Every Japanese man, woman, and child, 110,000 of them, was sent to inland prison camps. Even though the Japanese had been living in the United States since 1869, they were never allowed to become citizens. Suddenly, they were a people with no rights who looked exactly like the enemy.

With the closing of the prison camps in the fall of 1945, the families were sent back to the West Coast.

The Japanese relocation program, carried through at such great cost in misery and tragedy, was justified on the ground that the Japanese were potentially disloyal. However the record does not show a single case of Japanese disloyalty or sabotage during the whole war.

In June 1952, Congress passed Public Law 414, granting Japanese the right to become United States citizens.

Student Responses

Low   –   High   (Circle number)
1   2   3

PREDICTION:
Title   1   2   3
What do you think is meant by this title?

_____

_____

_____

RETELLING:
Character(s)   1   2   3
What happened to the people in this story?

_____

_____

_____

Problem(s)   1   2   3
Why were these people treated this way?

_____

_____

_____

Outcome(s)/Solution(s) 1   2   3
What happened after the war?

_____

_____

_____

SCORING GUIDE

TOTAL SCORE _____		Prompting		Reading Level	
10–12	Comprehension excellent	None	_____		
6–9	Comprehension needs assistance	General	_____	IND	_____
5 or less	Comprehension inadequate	Specific	_____	INST	_____
		Suggestive	_____	FRUST	_____

GLOSSARY OF KEY TERMS

- **Comprehension:** The process of constructing meaning from print.
- **Context Reader:** A student whose decoding skills are inadequate but who can usually answer questions based on the words decoded and background knowledge of the material.
- **Decoding:** Using a variety of skills, including phonics, to determine the spoken equivalent of a printed word.
- **Frustration Level:** The level at which adequate functioning in reading breaks down. Word recognition accuracy drops to 90 percent or lower. Comprehension is at 50 percent or lower. Only one of the two conditions needs to be met for a student to be at the frustration level—word recognition and/or comprehension.
- **Informal Reading Inventory:** A set of graded word lists and passages used to estimate students' oral and silent reading skills.
- **Independent Level:** Adequate functioning in reading with no help from the teacher. Adequate functioning means 99 percent accuracy in word recognition and 90 percent comprehension or better.
- **Instructional Level:** Adequate functioning in reading with help from the teacher. Adequate functioning means 95 percent accuracy in word recognition and 75 percent comprehension or better.
- **Listening Capacity Level:** Adequate understanding of the material that is read to the student by the examiner. A score of 70 percent or better is an indication of adequate understanding.
- **Miscue:** An oral reading response that is different from the correct response. It assumes that the reader is trying to make sense of what is being read. Miscues are not random errors.
- **Norm-Referenced Tests:** Tests that compare students with a representative sample of others who are the same age or in the same grade. The scores indicate whether students did as well as the average, better than the average, or below the average. These tests are not a very good source of information for assessing students or planning classroom instruction.
- **Phonics:** Ways of teaching children sound-symbol relationships to help them sound out words.
- **Predictions:** Guesses or inferences made on the basis of prior knowledge.
- **Readability:** An estimate of the difficulty level of text.
- **Reader Response Format:** A format that follows the type of literacy program that challenges students to use their inferential and critical reading and thinking abilities.
- **Reading Levels:** See Independent Level, Instructional Level, Frustration Level and Listening Capacity Level.
- **Structural Analysis:** Ways of teaching children how to break up longer words into pronounceable units.
- **Subskills Format:** Format that enables the teacher to diagnose a student's ability to decode words both in isolation and context and to answer questions.
- **Word Caller:** A student who is quite proficient at decoding words but does not assign meaning to the words decoded.
- **Word Recognition:** The ability to determine the oral equivalent of a printed word. It does not involve determining word meaning. The reader can recognize the word without knowing its meaning.

GLOSSARY OF BASIC DECODING TERMINOLOGY

- **Consonants:** All the letters of the alphabet except the vowels.

- **Consonant Blends:** Two- and three- letter consonant clusters in which each consonant letter retains some of its regular consonant sound; e.g., say the word *blend;* you should be able to hear both the *b* sound and the *l* sound.

- **Consonant Digraphs:** Sound made when two consonant letters are joined together. For example, the consonant *t* has its own sound as in *top* and *h* has its own sound as in *help*. However, when *t* and *h* are joined in a word such as *them,* a new sound—a consonant digraph—is produced. *Th, wh, ch, ng,* and *sh* are five of the most common consonant digraphs.

- **Fluency:** Reading in an expressive manner without any significant word recognition difficulty.

- **Grapheme:** A letter or letters that represent a speech sound.

- **Phoneme:** A sound in a language.

- **Phoneme-Grapheme Correspondence:** The association between a sound (phoneme) and the letter (grapheme) that represents it.

- **Prefix:** A beginning syllable that modifies the meaning of a word usually called a root word; e.g., *re* (again), the prefix, plus *start,* the root word = *restart,* to start again. See also Root Word and Suffix.

- **Rime:** A vowel and any following consonant of a syllable; e.g., *at* as in *cat, ike* as in *bike.*

- **Root Word:** A word of usually one or two syllables to which prefixes and suffixes are added; e.g., the root word *play* + the prefix *re* + the suffix *ed* = *replayed.*

- **Sight Word:** A word that is recognized instantly and automatically on sight as a whole word and without phonetic analysis; e.g., *the, and.*

- **Suffix:** Letters added after a root word to change the meaning of the word; e.g., the suffixer + the root word *read* = the noun *reader.*

- **Syllable:** A group of letters containing only one vowel sound; e.g., *paper* is a two-syllable word—*pa / per.* Only one vowel per syllable.

- **Vowels:** Sounds represented by the letters, *a, e, i, o, u,* and sometimes *y* and *w.*

- **Vowel Digraphs:** Two vowels grouped together in which one sound, most often the long sound of the first vowel, is heard and the second vowel is silent; e.g., *bead, soak.* Teachers refer to this as "When two vowels go walking, the first one does the talking."

- **Vowel Diphthongs:** Sounds that are the blending of the vowel sounds; e.g., *oi* as in *spoil, oy* as in *toy, ou* as in *loud, ow* as in *crown, au* as in *August, aw* as in *flaw.*

Inventory Administration Kit

SUBSKILLS FORMAT
FORM A: PRETEST

PART 1 Graded Word Lists

Form A: Pretest   Graded Word Lists

1.	this	1.	came
2.	her	2.	day
3.	about	3.	big
4.	in	4.	house
5.	are	5.	after
6.	you	6.	saw
7.	see	7.	put
8.	all	8.	under
9.	like	9.	went
10.	blue	10.	must
11.	my	11.	please
12.	said	12.	many
13.	was	13.	trees
14.	look	14.	boy
15.	go	15.	good
16.	come	16.	girl
17.	with	17.	ran
18.	away	18.	something
19.	bank	19.	little
20.	on	20.	saw

Form A: Pretest   Graded Word Lists

1.	fly	1.	birthday
2.	leg	2.	sing
3.	feet	3.	it's
4.	hear	4.	beautiful
5.	food	5.	job
6.	think	6.	elephant
7.	hat	7.	cowboy
8.	ice	8.	branch
9.	letter	9.	asleep
10.	green	10.	mice
11.	outside	11.	corn
12.	happy	12.	baseball
13.	less	13.	garden
14.	stop	14.	hall
15.	giving	15.	best
16.	grass	16.	blows
17.	street	17.	cold
18.	page	18.	law
19.	walk	19.	bat
20.	let's	20.	found

Form A: Pretest   Graded Word Lists

1.	distant	1.	drain
2.	phone	2.	jug
3.	turkeys	3.	innocent
4.	about	4.	relax
5.	clean	5.	goodness
6.	foolish	6.	seventeen
7.	engage	7.	disrespect
8.	show	8.	frown
9.	unhappy	9.	compass
10.	better	10.	attractive
11.	court	11.	fabric
12.	energy	12.	lettuce
13.	passenger	13.	operator
14.	start	14.	multiplication
15.	vacation	15.	violet
16.	pencil	16.	settlers
17.	labor	17.	polite
18.	decided	18.	internal
19.	policy	19.	drama
20.	nail	20.	toothbrush

Form A: Pretest   Graded Word Lists

1. moan	1. brisk
2. hymn	2. nostrils
3. bravely	3. compromise
4. voyage	4. headlight
5. shrill	5. hypothesis
6. jewel	6. farthest
7. chocolate	7. wreath
8. register	8. emptiness
9. classify	9. billows
10. graceful	10. mob
11. cube	11. calculate
12. scar	12. harpoon
13. muffled	13. pounce
14. pacing	14. rumor
15. toe	15. dazzle
16. guarantee	16. relationship
17. thermometer	17. hearth
18. erode	18. international
19. salmon	19. ridiculous
20. magical	20. widen

Form A: Pretest   Graded Word Lists

1.	proven	1.	utilization
2.	founder	2.	valve
3.	motivate	3.	rehabilitate
4.	glorify	4.	kidnapper
5.	adoption	5.	offensive
6.	darted	6.	ghetto
7.	nimble	7.	bewildered
8.	sanitation	8.	discourse
9.	enthusiastic	9.	vanity
10.	unravel	10.	radiant
11.	pompous	11.	horrid
12.	knapsack	12.	vastly
13.	bankruptcy	13.	strenuous
14.	geological	14.	greedy
15.	stockade	15.	sanctuary
16.	kerchief	16.	quartet
17.	snarl	17.	miser
18.	obtainable	18.	indignant
19.	hysterical	19.	scallop
20.	basin	20.	gradient

SUBSKILLS FORMAT
FORM A: PRETEST

PART 2 Graded Paragraphs

THE PLAY CAR

Tom has a play car.

His play car is red.

"See my play car," said Tom.

"It can go fast."

Ann said, "It's a big car."

"I like your car."

"Good," said Tom.

"Would you like a ride?"

OUR BUS RIDE

The children were all talking.

"No more talking, children," said Mrs. Brown.

"It is time for our trip."

"It is time to go to the farm."

Mrs. Brown said, "Get in the bus."

"Please do not push anyone."

"We are ready to go now."

The children climbed into the bus.

Away went the bus.

It was a good day for a trip.

MARIA'S PUPPIES

Maria has two puppies.

She thinks that puppies are fun to watch.

The puppies' names are *Sissy* and *Sassy*.

Puppies are born with their eyes closed.

Their ears are closed, too.

This is why they use their smell and touch.

After two weeks, puppies begin to open their eyes and ears.

Most puppies can bark after four weeks.

Maria knows that *Sissy* and *Sassy* will grow up to be good pets.

HOMEWORK FIRST

Marco and his sister Teresa love to watch TV.

The shows they like best are cartoons.

Every day after school they go outside to play.

Soon, Mother calls to them to come in.

"It's time to do your homework," she says.

"When you finish your homework you can watch your cartoons," Mother promises.

"Remember! Homework first."

Marco and Teresa are happy with this.

They do their homework.

Now they are ready to watch their cartoon shows.

LOOK AT THE SKY!

"Look at that sky!" shouted Sammie as he pointed upward. Suddenly a funnel like a monster's tail dropped out of the heavy clouds. Sammie grabbed Max's hand and yelled, "Run to the bridge! It's a tornado!"

Now The wind sounded like cattle chasing them. Sammie remembered the fear he'd felt when a farm steer had charged him. A cowboy had pulled him to safety. Now he was the brave cowboy.

Max saw the funnel on the ground. Leaves, branches and grass tumbled in the air around them. There it was! The bridge was within sight! Sammie and Max threw themselves under it. Sammie covered Max's body and held onto rocks. The wind screamed and pounded them, and then it was still.

Were they alive? He knew they had escaped when Max threw his arms around his neck. Max hugged Sammie with all his might.

THE GOAT HERDER

Mr. Hezbah drove his dairy goats over the dry African path. Seth awakened with the coming of the bleating goats in the morning. The little bells around their necks chimed. Seth longed to go with Mr. Hezbah. Mr. Hezbah was old and bent, and Seth wanted to help him.

Perhaps Mr. Hezbah would pay him with a young female goat in the spring. Perhaps he could raise the goat to produce milk. Perhaps he would sell the goat milk to buy clothes and supplies to attend school. Yes, he decided with a laugh, one little goat could change his life.

Seth saw Mr. Hezbah and the goats turn the bend. He said in his strongest voice, "Good morning, Mr. Hezbah! I am very good with animals. May I help you herd the goats? Mr. Hezbah stopped and smiled. Would this be the day that changed Seth's life?

IF GIVEN THE OPPORTUNITY

Mae Carol Jemison was born in 1956. Her parents, a carpenter and a teacher, had high hopes for her. But she was to achieve more than they ever imagined.

Young Mae Jemison had a passion to be a pioneer beyond the earth's horizon. Mae also had interests including dance, acting, and civil rights, both in high school and college. She achieved degrees in chemical engineering and medicine. Later, she practiced medicine in Africa.

After these accomplishments, Dr. Mae Jemison decided to pursue her childhood dream. She was one of 15 people chosen to become astronauts from a field of over 2,000. Dr. Jemison became the first African American woman ever admitted into the U.S. astronaut program. She flew into space aboard the U.S. Space Shuttle *Endeavour* on September 12, 1992.

Following her historic flight and fame, Mae Jemison said that society should recognize how much all individuals can contribute if given the opportunity.

BORN A SLAVE

He was born a slave on a farm in Missouri. When he was still a baby, his father was killed in an accident. His mother was kidnapped by night raiders. As a child, he was raised by Moses and Susan Carver. They were his owners. They named him George Washington Carver.

Mr. and Mrs. Carver taught George to read and write as a boy. He was very eager to learn, and showed a great interest in plants. When he was eleven years old he went to a school for black children in Neosho, Missouri.

For the next 20 years, Carver worked hard to pay for his education. George became a scientist and won worldwide fame for his agricultural research. He was widely praised for his work with peanuts. He found over 300 uses for peanuts. He also spent a great deal of time helping to improve race relations.

Carver got many awards for his work. The George Washington Carver National Monument was established on 210 acres of the Missouri farm where he was born.

THE OLD ONES

There is only one place in the United States where four states meet. It is the vast Four Corners region where Arizona, Colorado, New Mexico, and Utah come together.

The Four Corners region is a beautiful landscape of canyons, of flat mesas rising above broad valleys. It is slickrock desert and red dust and towering cliffs and lonely sky.

About 2,000 years ago, a group of men and women the Navajo people call the *Anasazi* moved into this area. *Anasazi* is a Navajo word; it means "the Old Ones."

At first, the Anasazi dug out pits, and they lived in these "pit" houses. Later, they began to build houses out of stone and adobe called *pueblos*. They built their pueblos in and on the cliffs.

The Anasazi lived in these cliff houses for centuries. They farmed corn, raised children, created pottery, and traded with other pueblos.

These once great pueblos have been empty since the last years of the thirteenth century, for the Anasazi walked away from homes that had been theirs for 700 years.

Who were the Anasazi? Where did they come from? Where did they go? They simply left, and the entire Four Corners region lay silent, seemingly empty for 500 years.

ALIENS IN THE EVERGLADES

Not long ago, a group of very surprised tourists suddenly came face-to-face with an alligator wildly fighting a large Burmese python in the Florida Everglades. Ten feet long, the native alligator battled against the bigger snake. Fully grown, these snakes can weigh 300 pounds and are over 17 feet long.

Burmese python first appeared in the Everglades in 1995. Many think that they were freed in this park by their owners. Others believe that they escaped pet stores and homes during Hurricane Andrew in 1992.

Alien species like the python do not have natural enemies in their new homes. They are a danger because they disrupt the food chain. Ultimately, it may be impossible to get rid of environmental troublemakers like the python once they have established themselves in a new habitat.

Many other incompatible species have escaped to the wild of the Everglades, including parakeets, swamp eels and squirrel monkeys. Consequently, Florida now also has more exotic lizard species than there are native lizards in the entire Southwest United States.

SUBSKILLS FORMAT
FORM A: POSTTEST

PART 1 Graded Word Lists

Form A: Posttest   Graded Word Lists

1.	to	1.	three
2.	now	2.	find
3.	so	3.	because
4.	from	4.	who
5.	big	5.	their
6.	had	6.	before
7.	at	7.	more
8.	yellow	8.	turn
9.	of	9.	think
10.	three	10.	yes
11.	no	11.	these
12.	jump	12.	school
13.	but	13.	word
14.	has	14.	even
15.	if	15.	would
16.	as	16.	like
17.	have	17.	ride
18.	be	18.	white
19.	or	19.	never
20.	an	20.	your

Form A: Posttest   Graded Word Lists

1.	maybe		1.	sound
2.	pass		2.	climb
3.	out		3.	waiting
4.	they		4.	hands
5.	please		5.	cry
6.	love		6.	doctor
7.	going		7.	people
8.	eight		8.	everyone
9.	kind		9.	write
10.	read		10.	inch
11.	paid		11.	green
12.	over		12.	before
13.	top		13.	thirty
14.	pool		14.	dance
15.	low		15.	test
16.	thank		16.	hard
17.	every		17.	don't
18.	short		18.	story
19.	just		19.	city
20.	us		20.	wash

Form A: Posttest   **Graded Word Lists**

1.	computer	1.	spy
2.	laugh	2.	downtown
3.	energy	3.	tray
4.	choice	4.	skull
5.	hospital	5.	exhibit
6.	court	6.	formal
7.	heard	7.	weekend
8.	closet	8.	nineteen
9.	together	9.	mixture
10.	picnic	10.	invitation
11.	eight	11.	volunteer
12.	law	12.	gulf
13.	build	13.	rumble
14.	objects	14.	plot
15.	probably	15.	cotton
16.	shark	16.	weary
17.	we'll	17.	faucet
18.	paragraph	18.	conversation
19.	telephone	19.	weep
20.	today	20.	jelly

Form A: Posttest   Graded Word Lists

1.	solution	1.	vibrant
2.	exercise	2.	greatness
3.	funeral	3.	tardy
4.	practice	4.	doughnut
5.	mutual	5.	optimist
6.	surrounded	6.	nurture
7.	deliberately	7.	dismay
8.	officially	8.	shipment
9.	taxi	9.	logic
10.	parachute	10.	reinforce
11.	radar	11.	fingerprint
12.	intermediate	12.	jumbo
13.	embarrass	13.	ballot
14.	heart	14.	narrator
15.	crude	15.	crutch
16.	bakery	16.	shopper
17.	knelt	17.	punish
18.	endure	18.	silken
19.	painful	19.	omelet
20.	squash	20.	predicament

Form A: Posttest   Graded Word Lists

1. noisily	1. duly
2. pyramid	2. furnishing
3. grieve	3. emptiness
4. foothills	4. frustration
5. nominate	5. joyously
6. include	6. patriotic
7. formulate	7. devout
8. enact	8. seriousness
9. depot	9. affluent
10. illegal	10. federation
11. distress	11. youth
12. childish	12. selection
13. unfair	13. dismal
14. eliminate	14. somber
15. athlete	15. habitation
16. luggage	16. fling
17. historically	17. dungeon
18. uncertainty	18. hierarchy
19. gardener	19. replica
20. enchant	20. journalist

SUBSKILLS FORMAT
FORM A: POSTTEST

PART 2 Graded Paragraphs

FISHING

Bob and Pam went fishing.

Bob put his line in the water.

He felt something pull on his line.

"A fish! A fish!" said Bob.

"Help me get it, Pam."

Pam said, "It's a big one."

Bob said, "We can get it."

JOSÉ'S FIRST AIRPLANE RIDE

José and his papa went to the airport.

José was very happy.

His papa was happy, too.

They got on the airplane.

Up high into the sky they flew.

"How high we are," said José.

"The cars look so small."

"And so do the houses," said Papa.

José said, "This is so much fun."

PLANT SPIDERS

There are all kinds of spiders.

Some spiders are big, and some spiders are small.

One kind of spider is called a plant spider.

Plant spiders are black and green in color.

Plant spiders have eight legs.

All spiders have eight legs.

Plant spiders spin their webs on plants.

That is why they are called plant spiders.

They soon learn to hunt for food and spin their webs.

THE RODEO

It is a warm, sunny day. Many people have

come to the rodeo to see Bob Hill ride Midnight.

Bob Hill is one of the best cowboys in the rodeo.

Midnight is one of the best horses in the rodeo.

He is big and fast. Midnight is a strong black horse.

The people at the rodeo stand up.

They are all waiting for the big ride.

Can Bob Hill ride the great horse Midnight?

GREAT WALL OF CHINA

The Chinese began work on the Great Wall about 2,000 years ago. Over time, it became the largest wall ever built. The Great Wall is about 25 feet high with watchtowers used for lookout posts. The Great Wall is almost 4,000 miles long. It was built to keep China safe from invaders from the north.

For the most part, the Great Wall kept China safe from these enemies. However, the armies of the Mongol leader Genghis Khan did cross the wall 900 years ago and conquered most of China.

Today, the Chinese no longer use the wall for defense. Visitors from all over the world come to see the Great Wall and walk the path along its top.

The Great Wall of China is so big a structure that astronauts can see it as they orbit the earth.

MISS MILLY'S KITTY

Miss Milly was an elderly lady who lived in the oldest house in our neighborhood. This little house still had a barn in the back and a wood burning stove in the kitchen.

Miss Milly was quite a sight to see. She wore enormous purple hats and red paper flowers pinned to her apron. She sometimes looked like the scarecrow in her garden. Filled with energy, Miss Milly rode an odd bike made from pipes and old buggy wheels.

Wherever she went, Miss Milly brought along her pet chicken perched on her shoulder. Miss Milly called her chicken Kitty, and sometimes slipped us kids a warm, brown egg from her apron pocket.

This was long ago, but I still remember fondly my childhood friends, Miss Milly and a chicken named Kitty.

A CURIOUS MIND

Eleven-year-old Mario Molina leaned over his microscope. All kinds of creatures were moving under the lens that he could not see without the microscope. Soon he was working with a chemistry set and using his bathroom as a laboratory.

Years later, Mario was the first Mexican American to win a Nobel Prize in Chemistry. The Nobel Prize includes a large sum of money and a gold medal. It is one of the highest awards in the world. Mario was picked because of his discoveries about dangers of chemicals in the earth's ozone layer.

Young people have asked Dr. Molina what qualities they need to have to become scientists. "Most of all, you need to be curious and creative. You need to work hard and be patient. Most of all, enjoy what you do. If you are curious, creative, hard-working and patient, being a scientist will be fun and rewarding."

ALONG THE OREGON TRAIL

Today Missouri is in the central part of the United States. In 1800, it was not the center. In those days Missouri was on the edge of the frontier. Very few people had ever seen the great lands that lay to the west of Missouri.

In 1804, Captain Meriwether Lewis and William Clark set out from St. Louis to explore these lands. In November 1805, they reached the Pacific Ocean. The route they took later became known as the Oregon Trail.

When they returned, Lewis and Clark told many exciting stories about the West. This made other people want to make the West their home.

By the 1830s, settlers began making the long trip to the West. Missouri was the starting place for almost all these settlers. In the cities of Independence, St. Joseph, or Westport, they bought wagons, tools, and food for the two-thousand-mile trip. They went along the Oregon Trail through plains and deserts, over mountains, and across rivers.

TITANIC

The *Titanic* was the largest ship in the world. The *Titanic* was thought to be unsinkable.

On the night of April 14, 1912, the sea was calm, and the night was clear and cold. The *Titanic* was on its first trip from England to New York. The captain had received warnings of icebergs ahead. He decided to keep going at full speed and keep a sharp watch for any icebergs.

The men on watch aboard the *Titanic* saw an iceberg just ahead. It was too late to avoid it. The iceberg tore a 300-foot gash in the *Titanic*'s side. The ship sank in about 2½ hours.

Of the 2,200 passengers and crew, only 705 people were saved. They were mostly women and children.

In 1985, researchers from France and the United States found the *Titanic* at the bottom of the Atlantic Ocean. Sharks and other fish now swam along the decaying decks where joyful passengers once strolled.

THE DIARY

Anne Frank, a young Jewish girl, was born in Germany in 1929. A few years after Anne's birth, Adolf Hitler and the Nazi party came to power in Germany. Germany was in a great economic depression at the time, and Hitler blamed these problems on the Jews. To escape the persecution of the Nazis, Anne and her family, like many other Jews, fled to Holland. There in Amsterdam, Anne grew up in the 1930s and early 1940s.

For her thirteenth birthday, Anne received a diary. She began writing in it. In 1942, Hitler conquered Holland, and the Nazis soon began arresting the Jews to send them to concentration camps. Millions of Jews died in these camps.

To escape the Nazis, the Franks went into hiding. Some of their Dutch friends hid Anne and her family in secret rooms above a warehouse in Amsterdam. In that small space the Franks lived secretly for more than two years. During that time, Anne continued to write in her diary.

By the summer of 1944, World War II was coming to an end. The American and British armies freed Holland from the Nazis, but not in time to save Anne and her family. Police discovered their hiding place and sent Anne and her family to concentration camps. Anne Frank died in the camp at Bergen-Belsen in March 1945. She was not yet sixteen years old.

All of the Franks died in the camps except Anne's father. After the war, Mr. Frank returned to Amsterdam. He revisited the small, secret rooms his family had hidden in for so long. Among the trash and broken furniture, he found Anne's diary.

READER RESPONSE FORMAT
FORM B: PRETEST

Graded Paragraphs

IT'S MY BALL

Tom and Nancy went for a walk.

They saw a small ball on the grass.

They began fighting over the ball.

While they were fighting, a dog picked up the ball and ran.

The kids ran after the dog, but the dog got away.

FISH FOR SALE

Susan got ten fish and a tank for her birthday.

She loved the fish and learned to take good care of them.

One day, Susan saw six new baby fish in the tank.

The fish tank was too small for all of the fish.

Dad said he would buy another tank for the baby fish.

Everyone began giving Susan fish and equipment.

Soon she had tanks for big fish, small fish, and baby fish.

Each tank had water plants, air tubes, and stones on the bottom.

Mom said, "Enough! Susan, your room looks like a store for fish."

That gave Susan an idea. Why not put all of the fish tanks in the garage and put up a sign?

Susan and her dad moved everything into the garage.

Susan made a big sign that read "FISH FOR SALE."

SILLY BIRDS

With food all around them, baby turkeys will not eat. They don't know food when they see it. They often die for lack of water. Water is always kept in their bowls, but some of these birds never seem to discover what the water is for. We have a hard time trying to understand these silly birds.

Baby turkeys don't know enough to come out of the rain either. So many of the silly young birds catch cold and die. If they see anything bright, they will try to eat it. It may be a coin, a small nail, or even a shovel. You can see how foolish these silly birds are.

ONE OF A KIND

"We found one," Kate whispered to her brother as they discover a deep burrow on the side of the pond. They had found a home of a platypus.

Tom and Kate are from Australia. So is the platypus. They have studied the platypus since they were children. These animals look a lot like ducks with fur. They are one of two mammals in the world that lays eggs.

Active at night, they live in the water and on land. They waddle when they walk, but they swim sleekly and smoothly. The animals dive for food on the bottom of streams, lakes and ponds. They have soft rubbery bills.

Platypuses find their prey using special detectors inside their bills. These detectors sense the tiny movements of their prey. Sharks are another water animal with these special detectors inside their mouths.

Tom and Kate wait in silence to watch for the platypus long after the sun has set. They see a platypus under the water swinging her head from side to side trying to find a meal.

THE FOX—A FARMER'S BEST FRIEND

"Meg, look! That's a female fox ready to have cubs." Uncle Mike was excited. "I haven't seen a fox around here for ten years." Meg said, "Shall I get your gun?" "There's no need for a gun," Uncle Mike replied. "Foxes help farmers by eating pests like mice, squirrels, frogs, and insects."

The next day Meg and her uncle were unhappy to learn that some farmers were hunting for the fox. These farmers didn't believe that a fox was helpful. Foxes save the farmers' crops by eating pests that destroy their crops. The farmers were sure that foxes only killed chickens and other small animals.

After weeks of hunting, the farmers gave up trying to kill the fox. When Uncle Mike and Meg found fresh fox and cub tracks on the far end of their farm, they were pleased the fox had not been killed.

HUSH MY BABY

Nate was a slave who lived with his master in Baltimore. Nate wanted freedom. He got an idea. "What if I build a big box, big enough so I could hide in it?" Nate got busy, and when the box was built, he got inside of it. Nate's uncle put the box on a ship that was going to New York. It was very cold in the box. Nate was afraid he would not make it to freedom.

On a Sunday morning, the ship arrived in New York. Nate's friend John was waiting at the dock. The ship's captain told John they didn't deliver boxes on Sunday. John worried that Nate might die from being in the box too long. He talked the captain into letting him take the box with him.

While the captain was helping John load the box onto a wagon, Nate sneezed. John was afraid that Nate would be discovered and sent back to his owner. To cover the noise of Nate's sneeze, John started singing "Hush My Baby." This also warned Nate to be very quiet. At last the box was delivered to the right house.

It was opened, and out popped Nate, cold and stiff—but happy and free!

THE HURT OF SHAME

Sticks and stones can break my bones, but words can never hurt me. Is this old rhyme true?

We all want people to see us as talented and special in some way. There are times we cannot be this ideal picture of ourselves or always be at our best. When those around us take notice, we can feel the hurt of shame.

This happens especially when we are blocked from something we want and enjoy, like friends and acceptance by others. It also can happen when we are thwarted from exciting or pleasing activities, such as making the sports team or being in the school band. We feel shame when our looks, clothes or achievements appear as being less.

In most cases, a broken bone can be healed, but not always a broken heart. Experiences of shame and their memory can hurt for a lifetime. The next time you see someone bullied or shamed, try to recall hurt feelings you yourself have experienced. Feel care and support for the victim. Helping people maintain their dignity and self respect helps heal the hurt of shame.

THE WORLD OF DINOSAURS

Before the 1800s, no one knew that dinosaurs had ever existed. Once in a while, people would find a dinosaur tooth or bone, but did not realize what it was.

When dinosaurs lived, the earth was not like it is today. Mountains like the Alps, for example, had not yet been formed.

The first dinosaur appeared on the earth about 220 million years ago. For 150 million years or so, they ruled the earth. Suddenly, about 63 million years ago, dinosaurs died out.

What caused this "terrible lizard," for that is what *dinosaur* means in English, to die out so suddenly?

Scientists have developed lots of theories to try to explain what happened to the dinosaurs. One theory is that the earth became too cold for them.

Most scientists believe that no single theory explains what happened to the dinosaurs. It may be that they could not keep up with the way the earth was changing. Whatever the cause, or causes, it was the end of the World of Dinosaurs.

READER RESPONSE FORMAT
FORM B: POSTTEST

Graded Paragraphs

THE RED ANT

The red ant lives under the sand.

The ant must build its own room.

It has to take the sand outside.

The sand is made into little hills.

Building a room is hard work.

The red ant is a busy bug.

WHY CAN'T I PLAY?

Kim wanted to play on the boys' team.

The boys said, "No."

One day, the boys needed one more player.

They asked Kim to play.

Kim got the ball and kicked it a long way.

She was a fast runner and a good player.

Todd, a boy on the team, kicked the ball to her.

Kim kicked the ball down the side of the field.

Tony, a boy on the other team, tried to block her.

He missed, and Kim scored.

Someone said, "Kim should have played on the team all year."

FLOODS ARE DANGEROUS

Mrs. Sánchez was driving home with her two sons, Luis and Ernesto. From the darkening sky, Mrs. Sánchez could see that a storm was coming. Soon, lightning flashed, thunder boomed, and the rain poured down. In order to get to her house, Mrs. Sánchez had to cross a road covered with water. She decided to drive across the rushing water. When they were just about across the road, the rising water caused the car to float away. Mrs. Sánchez knew that she had to get the boys and herself out of that car.

Luis was able to roll down the window and jump to dry ground. Mrs. Sánchez also jumped to dry ground. Mrs. Sánchez and Luis tried to grab Ernesto, but the car floated out of reach.

Soon the police and some friends came, and they searched all night for Ernesto and the car. They were unable to find them. Had Ernesto drowned in the flood, or was he safe?

Early the next day, Mrs. Sánchez saw a police car drive up to her house. Her heart raced when she saw Ernesto in the police car. He was safe! Ernesto told his mother that their car got stuck against a tree and that he was able to climb out of the car. He sat in the tree until daylight when the police found him. Everyone was happy to see Ernesto again.

FIRST TO DIE

It was very cold that March day in Boston. The year was 1770. It was a time of protest and riots. The people of Boston had had it with British rule.

Nobody knew that the day would end in bloodshed. This was the day of the Boston Massacre—March 5, 1770.

Somewhere in the city that night, a black man and former slave named Crispus Attucks was moving toward his place in history.

The British had brought troops into Boston in 1768. There were fights between the people of Boston and the soldiers.

On the night of March 6, 1770, the streets were filled with men. They were angry. Crispus Attucks was the leader of a patriot crowd of men. They met up with a group of British soldiers. The crowd pushed in on the soldiers. There was much confusion. A soldier fired his rifle. Attucks fell into the gutter—dead.

Crispus Attucks had been a leader in the night's actions. A black man and a former slave, he had helped to bring about action that led to the foundation of American independence.

TIGER

Tiger is hungry. He has not eaten for five days. His last meal was a wild pig. It is dark now, and Tiger is on a hunt. As he slinks through the jungle, the muscles of his powerful neck and shoulders are tense. Tiger senses that there are humans close by. Tiger is careful to avoid humans. He knows that only old or sick tigers will hunt humans because they are no longer swift enough to hunt other animals.

Suddenly, Tiger's sensitive nostrils pick up the scent of an animal. Tiger creeps slowly toward the smell. There, in a clearing in the jungle, he sees a goat. The goat has picked up Tiger's scent. Tiger moves in, but the goat does not flee. It is a trap! Humans have tied the goat there to trap Tiger. Tiger stops, then moves back into the jungle.

Tiger is hungry.

SENTINELS IN THE FOREST

Many wild creatures that travel with their own kind know by instinct how to protect the group. One of them acts as a sentinel.

Hidden by the branches of a low-hanging tree, I once watched two white-tailed deer feeding in a meadow. At first, my interest was held by their beauty. But soon I noticed something strange; they were taking turns feeding. While one was calmly cropping grass, unafraid and at ease, the other—with head high, eyes sweeping the sea marsh, and sensitive nostrils "feeling" the air—stood on guard against enemies. Not for a moment, during the half hour I spied upon them, did they stop their teamwork.

I LOVE A MYSTERY

Ever since the year 1841, when Edgar Allan Poe wrote *The Murders in the Rue Morgue,* people around the world have become fans of the mystery/detective story.

The mystery begins with a strange crime. There are a number of clues. A detective is called in to solve the mysterious crime. The clues may lead the detective to or away from the solution. In the end the detective reveals the criminal and tells how the mystery was solved.

The detective in most mystery stories is usually not a regular police officer, but a private detective. Probably the most famous of all these private detectives is Sherlock Holmes. With his friend and assistant Dr. Watson, Sherlock Holmes solved many strange crimes.

One of the most popular of all the mysteries that Holmes solved is called *The Hound of the Baskervilles.* In this story a man is murdered, and the only clue Holmes has to go on is an enormous hound's footprints found next to the dead man's body.

Do you love a mystery?

IT CANNOT BE HELPED

There is a phrase the Japanese use when something difficult must be endured—*it cannot be helped.*

On a quiet Sunday morning in early December 1941, the Japanese launched a surprise attack on Pearl Harbor. Shortly after that, the Army and the FBI began arresting all Japanese who were living along the West Coast of the United States. Every Japanese man, woman, and child, 110,000 of them, was sent to inland prison camps. Even though the Japanese had been living in the United States since 1869, they were never allowed to become citizens. Suddenly, they were a people with no rights who looked exactly like the enemy.

With the closing of the prison camps in the fall of 1945, the families were sent back to the West Coast.

The Japanese relocation program, carried through at such great cost in misery and tragedy, was justified on the ground that the Japanese were potentially disloyal. However the record does not show a single case of Japanese disloyalty or sabotage during the whole war.

In June 1952, Congress passed Public Law 414, granting Japanese the right to become United States citizens.